USAF F-105 THUNDERCHIEF
vs
VPAF MiG-17
Vietnam 1965–68

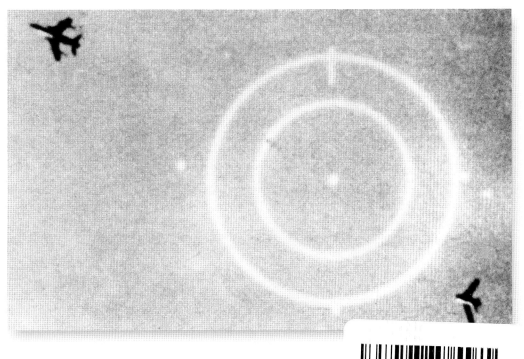

PETER E. DAVIES

OSPREY PUBLISHING
Bloomsbury Publishing Plc
PO Box 883, Oxford, OX1 9PL, UK
1385 Broadway, 5th Floor, New York, NY 10018, USA
E-mail: info@ospreypublishing.com
www.ospreypublishing.com

OSPREY is a trademark of Osprey Publishing Ltd

First published in Great Britain in 2019

A catalogue record for this book is available from the British Library.

ISBN: PB 9781472830906; eBook 9781472830890; ePDF 9781472830913;
XML 9781472830920

19 20 21 22 23   10 9 8 7 6 5 4 3 2 1

Edited by Tony Holmes
Cover artwork and battlescene by Gareth Hector
Three-views, cockpits, Engaging the Enemy and armament scrap views by
Jim Laurier
Maps and formation diagrams by Bounford.com
Index by Angela Hall
Typeset by PDQ Digital Media Solutions, Bungay, UK
Printed in China through World Print Ltd.

Osprey Publishing supports the Woodland Trust, the UK's leading woodland
conservation charity. Between 2014 and 2019 our donations are being spent
on their Centenary Woods project in the UK.

To find out more about our authors and books visit
www.ospreypublishing.com. Here you will find extracts, author interviews,
details of forthcoming events and the option to sign up for our newsletter.

Acknowledgments

Col "Jack" Broughton USAF (Ret), SSgt Neil Byrd USAF (Ret), Lt Col Robert
Cooley USAF (Ret), Maj Murray Denton USAF (Ret), Col Bill Hosmer
USAF (Ret), Capt John Nash US Navy (Ret), Dr István Toperczer, and
Col Boyd Van Horn USAF (Ret)

F-105 Thunderchief cover art

Capt Larry D. Wiggins was flying F-105D 61-0069 as "Hambone 3" in
a 469th TFS attack on the Bac Giang Bridge on June 3, 1967. After dropping
their bombs, the flight of four had just started to re-group when three silver
MiG-17s were seen climbing ahead to intercept them. The lead F-105D
(flown by Maj John Rowan) led the flight to meet them, turning through 180
degrees. The MiGs then set up a circular orbit at an altitude of 1,000ft, and
two F-105s tried unsuccessfully to break into the circle and fire Sidewinders at
the VPAF fighters. The MiGs' formation then changed to a wide "V" shape.
Wiggins, in full afterburner, dived at an angle of 20 degrees from an altitude
of 1,000ft and closed in behind the No. 2 MiG-17, which was 800ft below
him. He fired a Sidewinder from a range of 2,500ft just as the MiG pilot, Ngo
Duc Mai, lit up his afterburner and began a hard-left climbing turn. The
missile exploded about two feet from the MiG's tail. The 923rd FR machine
disintegrated, killing Mai. (Cover artwork by Gareth Hector)

MiG-17 cover art

On June 29, 1966 a flight of four camouflaged F-105Ds was engaged by four
silver MiG-17s during an *Iron Hand* (SAM site attack) as part of a major strike
by 32 F105s on a petrol, oil and lubricant storage facility 25 miles north of
Hanoi. Maj Fred Tracy flew as "Crab 2" in the *Iron Hand* flight in F-105D
58-1156. The MiGs were seen by two of the Thunderchief pilots, who then
broke away, and the Nos. 1 and 2 MiGs continued to pursue the remaining
two F-105s, approaching them from the left as they continued straight ahead.
As the MiGs approached from the rear, the F-105 leader (Maj Richard
Westcott in a two-seat F-105F) saw them. Jettisoning his own weapons, he
ordered Tracy to follow suit and then commenced a left turn in afterburner.
Capt Phan Van Tuc of the 923rd FR, flying a silver MiG-17, fired all three of
his guns, hitting Tracy's "Crab 2" with nine rounds as the USAF pilot began to
barrel roll in an attempt to get in behind the MiG. Tracy quickly succeeded in
doing so and shot down Tuc's aircraft – the first MiG kill credited to an F-105
pilot. (Cover artwork by Gareth Hector)

Previous Page

This dramatic frame from a Thunderchief's gun camera only hints at the
gut-wrenching life-and-death duel taking place between a MiG-17 and
another F-105D. Turning with MiG-17s in an aircraft that was as long as a
B-24 Liberator (but with more bombs and ten fewer crewmen) required
precise judgement to know when to disengage and accelerate away before the
adversary could get on the Thunderchief's tail. F-105 pilots could not easily
employ the tactic used by F-4 crews, which sought to draw MiG-17s into a
vertical fight where the Phantom II's superior thrust gave it a decisive
advantage. (USAF)

Contents

Introduction   4

Chronology   6

Design and Development   9

Technical Specifications   17

The Strategic Situation   29

The Combatants   36

Combat   50

Statistics and Analysis   72

Further Reading   78

Index   80

INTRODUCTION

The F-105 was designed as a bomber with both nuclear and conventional war-loads, although the dual racks seen here on the centerline of F-105B 57-5836 giving a total of 26 Mk 82 500lb bombs were not used operationally. The M61 Gatling gun in the nose of the B-model was moved aft in the F-105D. (USAF)

The F-105 and MiG-17 were very different aircraft, designed for disparate roles. It was ironic that the circumstances of the Vietnam War should bring the largest and most complex single-seat attacker of its time, effectively flying missions as a strategic bomber, into fighter-versus-fighter combat with one of the lightest, simplest and most maneuverable first-generation jet interceptors, operating within its optimum conditions. They each had single afterburning engines, one pilot (who in both cases regarded himself as a fighter pilot), a gun and sometimes a missile or two, but the differences outweighed the similarities.

Essentially, the USAF in 1965 was still equipped primarily for nuclear war, and conventional weapons capability was a secondary consideration in fighter-bomber design. F-105 pilots encountering MiGs over Vietnam usually had aircraft configured for bombing or surface-to-air missile (SAM) attack, and their attention and equipment was very focused on those roles. However, they could become effective air-to-air fighters, losing six aircraft to MiG-17s but

destroying 27.5 in return. Quickly resetting weapons switches and bombsights for air-to-air combat, or maneuvering to engage MiGs when encumbered with ordnance or drop tanks often proved too difficult in the heat of battle, almost certainly costing several MiG kills.

MiG-17 pilots flew less versatile fighters but they had other advantages. Their jets were nimble and heavily armed for close-in interception and combat. US Navy pilot Capt John Nash managed the *Have Idea* program in which MiGs were tested against US fighters in simulated dogfights. He concluded that, "the MiG-17, flown by a proficient air combat pilot, is very difficult to beat. It can enter a 6g turn at 375 knots and not lose more than 10 knots of airspeed in a 360-degree turn at full power. Don't ever try to outturn the MiG-17," but "at speeds over 400 knots it has an incredibly poor roll rate – less than 30 degrees per second. Roll rate is reduced severely the faster it goes."

Many VPAF pilots were less experienced than their USAF counterparts, but they fought above their own territory near their bases with excellent ground-controlled interception (GCI) and early warning of incoming attackers. Their instructors often had combat experience against US fighters, while their own powerful political motivation enabled them to face superior forces with tenacity for up to nine years of service.

There were many differences and inequalities between the rival fighter forces, but in aerial combat most of the rules dating back to World War I still applied, and these frequently decided the outcome of aerial duels over North Vietnam.

Built for short-range point defense, the MiG-17F "Fresco-C" relied on its heavy cannon armament, with a minimal external bomb-load which the VPAF used for a few wartime anti-shipping missions. It was not a fighter to underestimate, with legendary fighter ace Col Robin Olds labeling it a "vicious little beast." He also rated the majority of its pilots as skilled and aggressive. This particular example was flown by the VPAF's ranking MiG-17 ace, Nguyen Van Bay, and it is seen here on display in the courtyard of Dong Thap Museum in Cao Lanh city. Bay was born in the nearby village of Hoa Thanh, South Vietnam, in 1936. (István Toperczer)

CHRONOLOGY

1945

August Soviet scientists, like their contemporaries in Great Britain and the USA, become aware of advanced German research into swept-wing jet fighters. The MiG-8 light aircraft, testing swept wings and a canard tail, is flown in August 1945.

Summer North American designers use the German research to develop a swept-wing version of their FJ-1 Fury jet fighter, the F-86 Sabre.

1946

September Prime Minister Clement Attlee's Labour government agrees to a Soviet request for 25 Roll-Royce Nene 1 turbojets, and relevant blueprints, on condition that they are not used for military purposes.

April The MiG-9, Mikoyan's first jet fighter, flies using two copied BMW 003 turbojets.

1947

October The XP-86 Sabre prototype makes its first flight.
The Soviet Union receives 55 more Nenes but reneges on the non-military deal and copies the engine as the Klimov RD-45 and VK-1 for its MiG-15. More than 39,000 unlicensed copies are manufactured, with China continuing production into 1979.

1948

December The first production MiG-15 flies and 13,131 are eventually built in the Soviet Union, with others manufactured in Poland, Czechoslovakia and China.

1949

Fall Republic Aviation builds the swept-wing F-84F version of its Thunderjet fighter.

1950

January The SI-2 (MiG-17 prototype) flies.

The second YF-105A, 54-0099 completed its first flight on January 28, 1956. Although it lacks the four-petal airbrake arrangement, extended vertical stabilizer and forward-swept intakes of the F-105B, the basic Thunderchief shape is already evident. (USAF)

1951
August   MiG-17 production begins and 10,824 are built (including Polish manufacture and Chinese Shenyang J-5 versions) for more than 40 air forces.

1952
February   Republic Aviation submits its APX-63-FBX design that becomes the F-105A Thunderchief strike fighter.

September   199 F-105As are ordered.

1953
July   Soviet Air Forces (VVS) MiG-17s enter combat, shooting down a USAF RB-50 Superfortress in Soviet airspace.

December   The F-105 project is suspended.

1954
December   The F-105 is revived with the J75 engine, a new MA-8 fire control system (FCS) and an in-service date of 1958.

1955
October 22   The first YF-105A flies.

1956
March   North Vietnamese pilots begin basic training in the USSR and China.

May   The first F-105B flies.

1957
November   The USAF conceives the F-105D with the Thunderstick FCS.

1958
May   F-105Bs enter service but acceptance trials continue. The USAF orders 383 F-105Ds and 89 two-seat versions. To reduce costs, the USAF briefly proposes cuts, including the M61 cannon, fire suppression systems for the fuel tanks and all ECM provision.

1959
June 9   The first F-105D flies.

1960
February   In China, 52 Vietnamese Peoples' Air Force (VPAF) pilots begin conversion training to the MiG-17.

1961
March   The first operational F-105D is delivered and 14 Tactical Air Command (TAC) F-105 wings are planned.

1962
May   F-100 Super Sabre units in Japan and West Germany transition to the F-105D.

December   The first trained VPAF pilots return to North Vietnam.

Simplicity was the keynote of the MiG-15 and MiG-17 design philosophies. "Fresco-A" "Blue 61" was used to train North Vietnamese pilots at Kushchovskaya AB, in the Soviet Union, in the summer of 1964. (István Toperczer)

1964

February	The VPAF establishes its first fighter squadron, the 921st Fighter Regiment (FR), using 36 MiG-15UTIs and MiG-17s supplied by the USSR.
August	Yokota-based 36th Tactical Fighter Squadron (TFS) F-105Ds deploy to Korat, Thailand, after the Gulf of Tonkin Incident. They escort RF-101 reconnaissance aircraft and attack Pathet Lao AAA positions, losing one F-105D.
December 15	F-105Ds begin strikes on Laotian targets in Operation *Barrel Roll*.

1965

March 2	*Rolling Thunder* strikes begin, with 355th and 388th TFW F-105Ds as the principal attack aircraft.
April 3	921st FR MiG-17s enter combat, damaging a US Navy F-8E Crusader.
April 4	F-105 pilots encounter MiG-17s for the first time and two F-105Ds are shot down by the 921st FR – the first official US air-to-air losses of the war. F-105 pilots encounter MiGs on 151 occasions from April 4, 1965 to March 1, 1967.
April 9	Chinese MiG-17s shoot down a US Navy F-4B Phantom II.
June 24	MiGs attempt interceptions of F-105s.
September 7	A second VPAF MiG-17 unit, the 923rd FR, is formed.
October–November	MiGs attempt more interceptions of F-105s.

1966

April 23	MiG-17 interceptions of F-105 missions resume inconclusively.
May 10	A pursuit of a MiG-17 into Chinese airspace results in the first, but unofficial, shoot-down of a VPAF jet by an F-105.
June 29	A 388th TFW pilot claims the first official MiG-17 victory for the F-105. MiG-17 pilots develop better tactics.

	Two-seat F-105F *Wild Weasel* anti-SAM aircraft become a primary target for MiG-21 "Fishbeds."
July 19	F-105s and MiG-17s are involved in the longest dogfight of the war to date.
July 22	F-105s meet missile-armed MiG-17PFs.
September 4	MiG encounters become almost daily occurrences until January 1967. Large-scale dogfights take place as increased numbers of MiGs are launched to meet raids.
September 21	MiG-21s intercept US strike aircraft.
December 4	Four F-105Ds take on 16 MiG-17s. Seven F-105s have been lost to MiGs by year-end.

1967

March 10	Capt Max Brestel scores a double MiG-17 kill.
April	Nine more MiG-17 victories follow, with four on the 19th alone, when a second Medal of Honor is awarded to an F-105 pilot.
May	USAF F-105 and F-4 crews destroy 26 MiGs (six to F-105s), losing only two F-4Cs in return. MiG pilots tend to avoid F-105s during June and July, developing new ambush tactics.
August	MiG pilots return to the offensive, destroying several F-4Ds.
December	F-105F crews score the last two MiG kills for the Thunderchief. MiG activity is considerably reduced.

1968

January 5	F-105F from the 357th TFS becomes the last Thunderchief to fall to the MiG-17.
November 1	*Rolling Thunder* ends. F-105 activity shifts back to Laos.

DESIGN AND DEVELOPMENT

F-105 THUNDERCHIEF

Proponents of the F-105 responded to the increasing vulnerability of large bombers as enemy defenses introduced SAMs. Single-seat fighter-bombers, penetrating enemy defenses at high subsonic speed and low altitude, could each deliver devastating tactical nuclear weapons that became small enough to fit a fighter's internal bomb-bay. As the US Defense Department's emphasis shifted towards a more flexible response during the Kennedy era, the F-105D offered conventional weapons loads and its avionics gave the USAF much-needed all-weather attack capability.

When the Vietnam War began, the F-105 was TAC's primary strike aircraft. Its performance and hitting power appeared to offer rapid destruction of the enemy's limited military and industrial infrastructure. In practice, the war evolved very differently.

The Republic Aviation Corporation had provided the USAF with a series of tough, reliable fighter-bombers, including the P-47 Thunderbolt and the F-84 Thunderjet, 7,524 of which were manufactured in the early 1950s. Thunderjets flew ground-attack missions during the Korean War, introduced operational in-flight refueling and externally carried tactical nuclear weapons. A faster, swept-wing F-84F Thunderstreak derivative followed in 1950. All variants of the F-84 were underpowered, earning them the nickname "ground-hogs" due to their

The F-105B's increasingly complex avionics fit differentiated it markedly from the basic MiG-17. Many of the black boxes in this view are associated with the MA-8 FCS fire-control system. As the design progressed through later variants further equipment, and consequent weight increases, were continually added. (USAF)

long take-off runs – a consequence of slow powerplant development compared with unprecedented advances in airframe and avionics technology.

In 1951 the company's primary project for nine years became the delta-wing, Mach 3 XF-103 interceptor. Its extremely advanced Wright J67 turbo-ramjet engine and titanium structures presented insoluble problems, resulting in the $109m XF-103 venture being canceled in 1957 before the prototype stage.

Republic outlined a new fighter in 1952 with a more powerful engine and smaller nuclear weapons. Based on an enlarged RF-84F, the AP-63-FBX used a General Electric J73 turbojet to reach 800mph carrying 3,400lbs of nuclear weapons internally. With an Allison J71 replacing the J73, the design was supported by the USAF's Aircraft and Weapons Board in May 1952 and designated F-105, even though there was no specific requirement for such a machine. However, by September 1952, USAF interest generated a $13m contract for 199 J71-powered F-105As for service entry in 1955. This number was drastically cut to just 37 aircraft in March 1953.

The design had by then lost some of its F-84 characteristics, having a low-mounted tailplane, "clover leaf" airbrakes around the jet-pipe's rear end and a thin, mid-mounted wing swept at 45 degrees. Fixed, wing-root air intakes fed the J71, although development delays with that engine prompted its interim replacement with the successful 10,000lbs thrust Pratt & Whitney J57. Its armament of four 0.50in.-caliber T-130 machine guns was replaced by a 20mm T-171 (M61) revolver cannon at the suggestion of Gen Albert Boyd at the Wright Air Development Centre. An RF-105 reconnaissance version was proposed in August 1953.

The fairly basic airframe was progressively equipped with advanced avionics and systems until its increased weight and continued delays with the J71 caused suspension of the project. Interest was revived by the possibility of using the very powerful Pratt & Whitney J75, under development for the USAF's Convair F-106 interceptor. A limited contract for 15 F-105As was reinstated, although with the back-up options of the J57 and Wright J67 retained.

Typically for that period of military procurement, USAF requirements continued to change and the F-105 contract shrank to two J57-powered aircraft and one with a YJ75 in September 1954. In December, the USAF finally expressed confidence in the project, and in Republic, by effectively writing operational requirement GOR-49 around the F-105B specification. During 1954, a sophisticated, computer-managed FCS, in-flight refueling and a wide range of armament, including AIM-9 missiles, 2.75in. rocket pods and conventional bombs, were added. In January 1955 two J57-powered prototypes, ten YF-105Bs with YJ79s, and three YRF-105Bs (canceled in May 1956) were ordered, with any modifications resulting from flight testing to be incorporated on the production line.

The two YF-105As had RF-84F-style elliptical intakes with a smaller vertical tail and two-foot shorter fuselage than production models. Crucially, early flight tests in October–December 1955 showed serious deficiencies in supersonic performance. The air intakes were redesigned with an innovative forward-swept outline (similar to the XF-103's) but the performance shortfall, like the Convair F-102's, was compensated for by NACA Langley's discovery of area rule. By re-contouring the fuselage with distinctive "waisted" contours to redistribute pressure across its surface, transonic drag could be considerably reduced. Enlarged vertical tail and ventral fin surfaces improved directional stability – another common problem with the early "Century series" fighters.

After brief consideration of the J75-powered North American F-107 as an alternative to the still unproven F-105, the F-105B was ordered in quantity in January 1956 and the first J79-driven example flew on May 26. On July 25 it was officially named "Thunderchief," and after a protracted test period the 4th FW began to receive aircraft in May 1958. However, problems with the FCS, undercarriage, ejection seat and supersonic acceleration persisted throughout its Category III acceptance tests. The frequent modifications slowed production so much that the first USAF squadron did not receive its full 18-aircraft complement until 1960. Even then, reliability problems continued.

A formidable arsenal of external stores was also part of the F-105 specification from the outset. Here, an F-105B pilot stands guard over the "secret" cloth-shrouded (nuclear) stores and is surrounded by AIM-9Bs, an M61 and its 20mm ammunition and an array of free-flight rockets. M117 and Mk 82 bombs, practice bomb dispensers, fuel and napalm tanks are also lined up, together with a "buddy" in-flight refueling pod. (USAF)

The second YF-105A and the third F-105B (54-0102) test a USAF-sponsored "buddy" refueling system as one of the methods of extending a loaded Thunderchief's tactical radius. The F-105B is from the first batch of four test aircraft, and it retains the extra "rear view" windows (deleted on production F-105Bs) and extended nose boom, but it does have the extended vertical tail and area-ruled rear fuselage with four-petal airbrakes. (USAF)

19ft 8in.

F-150D THUNDERCHIEF

F-105D-10-RE 60-0497 of the 44th TFS/388th TFW was used by Maj Maurice "Mo" Seaver (who had the call-sign "Tamale 01") to attack Vinh Yen army barracks on May 13, 1967. As he pulled up from dropping his six 750lb bombs, Seaver saw a camouflaged MiG-17 ahead of him and fired 500 rounds of ammunition in two bursts, setting it on fire. He was credited with the aircraft's destruction, its pilot almost certainly being from the North Korean "Doan Z" group. Seaver's F-105D, nicknamed *MISS T*, was later shot down by a MiG-21 on November 18, 1967 – two Thunderchiefs fell to "Fishbeds" on this date.

34ft 9in.

USAF
00497

64ft 4.75in.

Emphasis quickly shifted to the F-105D, a 1957 initiative to combine the F-105B's spectacular performance with all-weather capability. A new radar required a 15in. fuselage extension and re-siting the M61 cannon rearwards to a position in the ammunition storage bay, with a new ammunition feed system. The nose then accommodated the AN/ASG-19 FCS and its R-14A radar. A General Electric FC-5 flight control system conferred substantial all-weather capability. After the first flight, extensive trouble-shooting tests had to be undertaken before production aircraft began to reach the 4520th Combat Crew Training Wing (CCTW) in March 1961.

Various two-seat F-105s were offered as proficiency trainers, initially the F-105C version of the F-105B and, in 1958, an F-105D-based two-seater, the F-105E. Both had a tandem bubble canopy in a fuselage of F-105D length. Finally, in June 1962, the USAF belatedly ordered a two-seat Thunderchief to assist new pilots' transition. The F-105F had a 36in. fuselage "plug" for a second cockpit with a separate canopy. Vertical tail area was increased by 15 percent and the undercarriage was reinforced to handle a 3,000lb weight increase. F-105Fs entered 4th TFW service in December 1963.

The F-105B's M61A1 cannon installation required 1,028 rounds of linked 20mm ammunition to be loaded into a supply box. The links were then fed into another container behind the gun, helping to maintain the center of gravity. A different feed and storage system was used in the F-105D. (USAF)

MiG-17

MiG designs, generated by the Soviet OKB-155 design bureau headed by Artyom I. Mikoyan and Mikhail I. Gurevich, originated before World War II. The company built high-altitude interceptors, including the piston-engined MiG-1 (based on an earlier Polikarpov design) and MiG-3 in 1939. Superior and more numerous fighters from Lavochkin and Yakovlev prompted more innovative MiG designs using mixed jet and piston engine or rocket powerplants in 1945.

MiG OKB produced the USSR's first jet-powered aircraft, the MiG-9, in 1946. This straight-winged interceptor with two 23mm guns and a single 37mm weapon entered limited service that same year. Following the unexpected gift of British Rolls-Royce Nene engine technology (also in 1946), OKB-155 began work on a more ambitious fighter to use this more reliable powerplant, renamed the Klimov VK-1.

German swept-wing technology was used in the resulting MiG-15 fighter, which bore some resemblance to Focke-Wulf's projected Ta 183 and the North American F-86 Sabre – the latter also based partly on German research. Faster than the straight-winged Allied jets that it met during the Korean War, the MiG-15's maneuverability, particularly at high altitude, exceeded the F-86's. Heavy armament, inherited from the MiG-9, made it a lethal bomber interceptor.

SHENYANG J-5 (MiG-17F)

36ft 5in.

12ft 5in.

31ft 7in.

Like the F-105, the MiG-17 had a rear fuselage section that could be pulled off for access to the engine. It extended from Frame 14 to Frame 28 of the fuselage structure and, like the rest of the fuselage, it consisted of a strong combination of traditional frames, longerons and stringers to support the V95 aluminum skin. Maintenance, underway here at the A-33 Repair Center in North Vietnam, was straight-forward and often consisted of battle damage repair. (István Toperczer)

With the MiG-17, the OKB sought to improve the MiG-15's performance with a new wing, swept at 45 degrees (like F-100 Super Sabre's) rather than 35 degrees. The bureau also drafted two versions, a tactical fighter and a radar-equipped all-weather interceptor. Since much of the original MiG-15 structure was retained, development of the "MiG-15bis 45°" (the wing-sweep angle) or I-330 proceeded swiftly. By February 1950 it was achieving 602 knots at 7,200ft and 582 knots at 33,460ft – a notable improvement on the MiG-15 with the same engine.

Tailplane flutter caused the loss of the first aircraft and its pilot, I. T. Ivashchenko, on March 20, 1950, and aileron reversal, due to lack of stiffness in the wing structure, occurred in the second prototype. The hardy simplicity of the design meant that flight-testing progressed faster than the far more sophisticated F-105's and, like the Thunderchief, production began in 1951 before testing was completed.

The only way of increasing the VK-1's thrust was by afterburning, tested in 1951 – bench-tests showed a 25 percent thrust increase. Afterburning was incorporated in production MiG-17Fs (NATO reporting name "Fresco-C") from late 1952, but it could only be ignited at a minimum altitude of 10,000ft and was not intended for a full afterburner take-off. Further improvements in service gave the MiG-17F an SRD-1 gun-ranging radar, installed ahead of the windscreen, a cooling system for the cockpit air conditioning and a fuel system that would not cut out under negative g for at least 15 seconds. Many one-off versions were built to test photo-reconnaissance and ordnance-delivery potential, including one with three vertically swiveling cannon in the nose, either for ground attack or to improve a pilot's firing angle on a target aircraft.

OPPOSITE

J-5 "Red 3012" was assigned to the 923rd FR at Kep in 1968. A number of MiGs were sprayed thinly with the dark green paint applied to Soviet military vehicles, mainly to help disguise them in their camouflaged storage areas outside the airfield perimeter. The temporary paint was also useful for hiding MiGs that patrolled at low altitude, awaiting a chance to ambush F-105s.

The MiG-17's two 23mm Nudel'man-Rikhter NR-23 (Norinco Type 23 weapons in the Chinese-built J-5) and single 37mm Nudel'man N-37D cannon, seen here, could be lowered from the fuselage as a gun pack. A built-in, hand-operated winch raised and lowered the gun tray, its ammunition boxes and link ejection ports for rapid rearming and maintenance. The guns were charged by a pneumatic mechanism and recharged by recoil action. (István Toperczer)

F-105 pilots had no two-seat trainer version of their aircraft until the F-105F was belatedly supplied to the 4th TFW at the end of 1963. VPAF pilots, however, had the benefit of around 80 hours of training on the two-seat MiG-15UTI prior to graduating to the MiG-17. They began training on Soviet examples in the USSR, although MiG-15UTIs and similar Shenyang JJ-5s were also supplied to the VPAF's 910th Julius Fucik Training Regiment in 1964 and used by the 921st and 924th FRs at Noi Bai throughout the war years. (István Toperczer)

MiG OKB began development of a night/all-weather MiG-17 variant in 1952, equipping some production-line examples with an RP-1 Izumrud radar set. This could easily be installed in the MiG's intake area, offering a search range of 6.48 nautical miles and automatic target-tracking at one nautical mile with minimal cockpit workload. The MiG-17P "Fresco-B" entered production in July 1953, and it was succeeded by the MiG-17PF "Fresco-D" (designated the Chengdu J-5A when built in China) with an afterburning VK-1F engine in December 1953. Performance was slightly inferior to the MiG-17F's due to the weight increase of 586lbs.

Chinese production of the MiG-17 included the Chengdu/Shenyang Jianjiao-5 or JJ-5 (MiG-17UTI) two-seat trainer, developed in 1964. It mated the MiG-15UTI's nose to a MiG-17 airframe with a non-afterburning VK-1A engine and a single NR-23 gun in a detachable belly pack. Around 1,000 were supplied to China's People's Liberation Army Air Force (PLAAF) from November 1967 until 1986, and examples were also used for training VPAF pilots in China.

TECHNICAL
SPECIFICATIONS

F-105 THUNDERCHIEF

The USAF used two F-105 variants in Vietnam, and both were heavily involved in combat with MiG-17s. The single-seat F-105D was the principal tactical striker during Operation *Rolling Thunder* and the F-105F was a two-seat strike fighter or, with ECM modifications, a *Wild Weasel* radar suppression platform. The developed F-105G variant added in-built jamming systems.

All versions had a Pratt & Whitney J75-P-19W axial-flow turbojet developing 16,100lbs thrust in military power and 24,500lbs in afterburner. The "W" in the engine designation indicated "water injection." Water was sprayed into the engine ahead of the first-stage compressor at 110psi, increasing the mass flow through the engine and cooling the turbine to allow for higher rpm. It briefly boosted take-off thrust to 26,500lbs until the 36-gallon water tank ran out.

The J75 engine proved to be extremely reliable in combat, absorbing damage and giving the aircraft sufficient speed and acceleration at low altitude to outrun almost all MiGs. Inevitably, the single-engine configuration lacked the "get you home" capability of the F-4 Phantom II's twin J79s, and a number of F-105s were lost through engine failure, particularly in the early days and often during, or soon after, take-off.

The F-105's considerable size was dictated partly by its massive engine and, consequently, numerous fuel tanks, and also by the 16ft-long internal bomb-bay for

its original primary mission as a nuclear striker. Its relatively conventional airframe was an evolutionary development of earlier Republic F-84 designs, but it introduced innovative swept-forward air intakes with internal hydraulically moveable plugs that provided a variable inlet area, matching the airflow to the engine's requirements across a range of speeds and altitudes. At Mach 1.92 the plugs were in the fully forward position, sliding on rails built into the intake walls and working in conjunction with automatic bleed-air doors. Two extra air inlet doors were located in the inner wheel-well walls, opening when the landing gear was lowered. A further air intake was located at the base of the vertical fin's leading edge, providing cooling air for the afterburner and rear fuselage interior.

Republic engineers were also innovative in their use of machine-milled skins, which varied in thickness depending on their load-bearing requirements, lightening the aircraft but still providing an airframe that could stand load factors of +8.67/-4.0g in subsonic maneuvering. In combat, F-105s regularly exceeded those limits.

In-flight refueling was vital for F-105 missions in Vietnam, and this 354th TFS/355th TFW pilot is using the drogue method, with a "basket" attached to the 12ft hose extending from a KC-135A's flying boom. Heading for the Than Hoa Bridge on April 3, 1965, this F-105D is carrying two AGM-12A Bullpup missiles. This mission was the first occasion on which MiG-17s were launched to challenge American aircraft, 46 F-105s forming the main strike force. (USAF)

At the end of the removable rear fuselage were four, 3ft-long, petal-type speed-brakes. They automatically opened by nine degrees when the afterburner was lit, giving a wider nozzle area. The two side petals could open fully when the undercarriage was lowered. A 20ft ring-slot braking parachute was housed behind the rudder's base.

The wings, mid-mounted and swept at 45 degrees like the MiG-17's, covered 385ft^2 in area compared with the MiG's 243ft^2. However, with a fuselage 67ft long (F-105F/G) compared with the MiG-17's 26.5ft, and a span of 34.75ft versus 31.5ft for the MiG, the Thunderchief's wing was comparatively small, limiting maneuverability. Critics of the aircraft's power-off capability (a contributing factor to its "Thud" nickname) may have been surprised that it could officially glide for 58 miles from 40,000ft.

The hydraulic system, an Achilles' heel in combat, used three independent systems. Two primary systems operated the flying controls, with one for each side of the aircraft, backed up by a ram-air turbine giving limited control of an emergency hydraulic system to power the "primary one" system. A separate utility system operated the undercarriage, flaps, speed-brakes, gun, brakes, variable inlet plugs, refueling probe and water injection pumps. All hydraulic lines ran close to each other in the lower fuselage, making them extremely vulnerable to damage by AAA. Modifications were made to improve survivability after numerous losses.

In-flight refueling, crucial for the F-105's role as a fighter-bomber that could be deployed easily to foreign crisis areas, was possible with either an extending refueling probe for drogue-type tankers or through a receptacle in the upper nose area for the Flying Boom method. In April 1965 pilots Maj Burriss Begley and Capt Thomas Hopkins relied on KC-135 tankers for their 5,730-mile flight, lasting for 9hrs 44mins, from Hawaii to Kadena AB, on Okinawa, in the *Two Buck Three* deployment by the 421st TFS. Begley was later shot down and killed by Nguyen Dang Kinh's MiG-21 during a December 5, 1966 *Iron Hand* mission after receiving a vague MiG warning.

The F-105D's primary all-weather nuclear strike role required far more sophisticated avionics than the MiG-17's. The suite included the ASG-19 Thunderstick integrated FCS, offering visual or "blind" weapons delivery and an air-to-air mode. The latter was included on the understanding that pilots might briefly encounter enemy interceptors en route to their targets, rather than as a dogfighting system. Thunderstick included an R-14A NASSAR search and ranging monopulse radar and a sophisticated AN/APN-131 Doppler navigation system with terrain avoidance, ground and contour mapping data on the pilot's five-inch cathode ray tube. Other avionics assets included AN/ARN-62 TACAN, AN/ARN-61 instrument landing system and AN/ARC-70 UHF command radio. Easy-to-read vertical tape cockpit instruments displayed speed and altitude data.

The F-105's original armament was one Mk 28 RE or Mk 43-1 parachute-retarded nuclear store carried internally and possibly two B61 or Mk 57s on external pylons. The emphasis on more flexible responses than all-out nuclear attacks called on the F-105D's capability to handle a range of conventional general purpose (GP) or cluster bombs, rocket pods and (for the F-105F/G) anti-radiation missiles. In a July 1963 firepower demonstration, two 357th TFS pilots each delivered 16 M117 750lb GP bombs, having taken off at a gross weight of more than 52,000lbs. For combat, a load of six M117s was more usual.

Provision was made for two Ford Aerospace/ Raytheon AIM-9B Sidewinder missiles, but the most useful air-to-air weapon, also used for ground attack, was the inbuilt General Electric M61A1 Vulcan 20mm rotary cannon. Most of the F-105's successful fights with MiG-17s were won with this "secondary" weapon, although an AIM-9B was also used for one of these gun kills and two others were missile-only victories.

A pair of M118 GP "bridge busters" await loading onto F-105D 61-0134 of the 357th TFS/355th TFW at Takhli RTAFB. The 3,000lb weapon contained a 1,975lb Tritonal warhead. With such a heavy bomb under each wing, the F-105 was in a serious asymmetric situation if one hung up. Indeed, several Thunderchief losses were attributed to this problem. (Neil Byrd)

Although a single AIM-9B missile may have seemed only token armament compared with the eight air-to-air missiles of an F-4 Phantom II, its presence had a deterrent effect. A second missile could be carried on the aircraft's other outboard pylon in place of an ECM pod. A dual launcher for two AIM-9Bs was produced, but it created excess drag and could not be jettisoned – "cleaning off" all external ordnance, including tanks, was normally an option if a pilot needed extra speed to escape from a faster MiG-21. With ordnance, the F-105's speed advantage over any MiG was significantly reduced.

AIM-9B Sidewinders sit ready for loading onto a 355th TFW F-105 at Takhli RTAFB. The missiles began to appear on Thunderchiefs in 1967 as the MiG threat grew. Sidewinders increased a pilot's range of air-to-air options, but circumstances often dictated that the gun was the more effective choice. (Neil Byrd)

There was also a perception that opportunities to use the missiles would be limited, and the F-105's five stores pylons could be better used for other weapons or pods. However, as the MiG threat increased, Sidewinders were carried on most missions over North Vietnam from December 1966 onwards, although they often appeared on only two aircraft in a flight while the others had two ECM pods.

As America's first mass-produced heat-seeking missile, the AIM-9B was part of the overall F-105 specification (and most other fighter projects) from December 1954 onwards following successful initial tests in September of the previous year. It offered greater simplicity and reliability than the costlier Hughes AIM-4 Falcon that was chosen for Air Defense Command interceptors.

Essentially, the weapon comprised a rocket motor and a 12.5lb blast-fragmentation warhead with a Mk 304 influence fuse, all in a tubular aluminum body 111.4in. long. In the nose, a lead-sulphide infra-red seeker was covered by a glass dome. Initial production versions had to be fired within a cone almost directly behind the target aircraft at a range of 3,000ft to 3,500ft. If the launch aircraft or the target maneuvered at more than 2g the AIM-9B would break lock and fly off ballistically. Sidewinders liked to "see" their targets against a clear sky background, and they could be distracted by the sun, by ground-heat if the target was in a dive or by clouds.

For a MiG-17 pilot with limited rearward visibility from his cockpit, keeping his aircraft maneuvering gently was essential if he was to see when a hostile missile was launched. He could then time a sharp, high-speed 70-degree turn or instigate a shallow dive so that his attitude relative to the missile was constantly changing. Either maneuver would usually break the AIM-9B's lock. The Thunderchief pilot's best chance of a successful missile launch was from directly behind the MiG-17, climbing into its blind spot with a clear sky background and the correct launch parameters.

In near textbook conditions the missile could perform well, as Majs Robert Rilling and Carl Osborne proved on May 13, 1967 when they each downed a MiG-17 with

QRC-160A ECM POD

As the aircraft most threatened by North Vietnamese SA-2 missiles, the F-105 was the first to use QRC-160A (ALQ-71) ECM pods in action. After unsuccessful use on equally vulnerable RF-101Cs, the Thailand-based F-105 units received pods from mid-1966. Used in the correct four-aircraft formations to maximize their effect and supported by EB-66C ECM aircraft, they became virtually essential for missions over North Vietnam by 1967, and they markedly reduced losses to SAMs. Usually the flight lead and element lead (aircraft No. 3) carried a pod on the right outboard pylon and an AIM-9B on the left outboard pylon. The two wingmen (Nos. 3 and 4) usually had two pods each. Horizontal spacing between aircraft was 500ft to 1,000ft depending on the pod configuration of the aircraft, and the formation had to be rigorously maintained to preserve the overall "blanket" of jamming. Pods were switched on when the Force Commander called "Start your music," and the pilot had only to monitor the indicator "fail" lights to ensure the pod was still working.

AIM-9B SIDEWINDERS

A single AIM-9B was the F-105's secondary means of self-defense, although the missile was used in only three of the Thunderchief's 27.5 MiG kills. However, as Col "Jack" Broughton observed, "We were always short of Sidewinders. If we had them, we loaded them. They were always nice to have in case you got on a MiG and had time to set up the switches to get the missile ready to fire." A twin launcher, as seen here, was tested on JF-105B 54-0112 to increase the "Thud's" defensive punch, but it proved to be too "draggy" and impractical for combat.

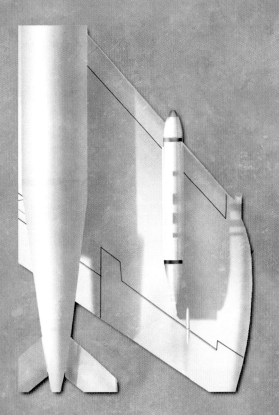

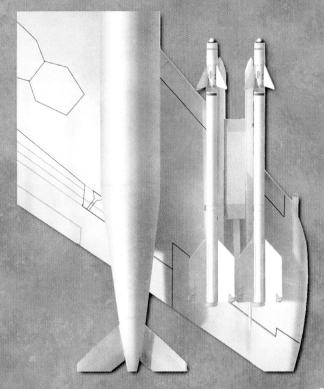

single AIM-9Bs. However, the Korat pilot whose missile went ballistic followed by a malfunctioning gun that emitted flames into his intake, stalling the engine, deserved sympathy for a missed MiG-21 kill opportunity on May 22, 1967 – possibly the closest an F-105 came to downing a "Fishbed."

Pilots sometimes complained that the missiles' seeker heads were scratched and abraded by debris and rain, reducing their ability to detect infrared targets. Later models, from the 1970s' AIM-9E/G/J onwards, offered greater flexibility in operation, leading to the all-aspect third-generation AIM-9L/M. F-105s used the AIM-9B throughout their time of conflict with MiG-17s. MiG-21s in turn used the K-13 "Atoll," which was an AIM-9B copy.

The Sidewinder's nagging unreliability meant that the M61A1 Vulcan cannon quickly became the Thunderchief pilot's preferred weapon when engaging MiG-17s. In the F-105D, the internal M61 cannon and its ammunition – the only fixed armament – weighed little more than 800lbs. The six-barrel unit, weighing 275lbs, fired M50 20mm ammunition at 6,000 rounds per minute with a muzzle velocity of 3,380ft per second in 2.5 second bursts, with cooling time between bursts. Although the total firing time was only ten seconds, a well-aimed burst of 100 rounds per second could literally saw the wing off a fighter.

The 1,028 conventionally linked rounds were stored in a cylindrical drum, and rearming was simplified by winching the drum from the aircraft's nose. The linked ammunition was later replaced by linkless rounds after problems with broken links at the high rate of firing achieved by the M61. Empty cases and links were returned to the drum after firing to preserve the center of gravity. A slotted gun-bay door was

F-105D/F CANNON

The General Electric T171 cannon fitted in the nose of the F-105 revived a late 19th-century design which added an electric motor to a "Gatling" rotary, multi-barrel gun. It entered production as the M61A1 in 1957, and its compactness, light weight and firing rate of up to 6,000 rounds per minute made it ideal for the F-104 Starfighter, F-105 Thunderchief and later fighters. In the F-105D, F and G, its 1,028 rounds of linkless 20mm ammunition (allowing about ten seconds of firing) were stored in a drum that also collected empty shell cases. The hydraulically powered gun weighed 275lbs – little more than half the weight of a full ammunition load.

retro-fitted to F-105D/Fs after combat revealed inadequate ventilation of the gun compartment. Only one AIM-9B missile was carried on many occasions, favoring the use of the gun as the primary weapon in a situation where only a solitary firing opportunity was likely to occur and complex switching was needed to change from "missiles" to "guns-air."

The K-19 reflector gunsight was sometimes unreliable, and Maj Kenneth T. Blank was one of many pilots who regretted its lack of ranging information. Like Capt Doug Lauck, Maj Fred Tracy and Blank's own wingman on the day of his MiG kill, Blank resorted to centering his target in the F-105's windshield, with some visual help from the pitot boom on the nose. For Tracy and Blank, who were among ten pilots to achieve MiG kills in this way, the technique worked adequately despite the highly concentrated route of the stream of shells from the gun. Because the gun focused so exactly on one small target area, pilots sometimes "stirred" their control column a little to disperse the shells. Against a non-maneuvering target, with a good operational gunsight, a pilot could direct his fire against a MiG's engine, fuel tank or cockpit.

The M61 itself was generally reliable despite the high rate of fire, with failures limited to around ten percent. However, jamming could occur if a round slipped out of place in the ammunition drum or on the conveyor belts. Jamming caused missed MiG kill opportunities on several occasions.

This official diagram shows how the General Electric M61A1 cannon was installed within the nose of the F-105D/F. The gun bay was purged by bleed air from the eighth-stage engine compressor, which drove gun-gas out through slots in the gun-bay door. The weapon was often used in conjunction with rockets against defended sites. Having selected "wing pylons" (rather than centerline bombs) and "rockets" on the armament panel, a pilot could set the same 48 mils depression on his gunsight reticule (rather than 128 mils for bombs) for guns and rockets. A burst from the M61A1 would then suppress defensive fire in the same pass as rocket firing. (USAF)

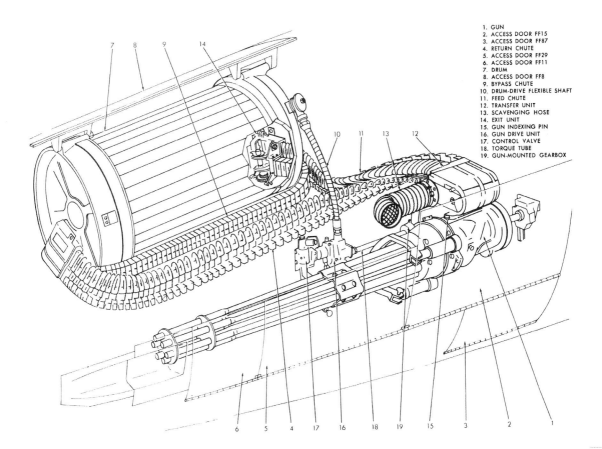

1. GUN
2. ACCESS DOOR FF15
3. ACCESS DOOR FF87
4. RETURN CHUTE
5. ACCESS DOOR FF29
6. ACCESS DOOR FF11
7. DRUM
8. ACCESS DOOR FF8
9. BYPASS CHUTE
10. DRUM-DRIVE FLEXIBLE SHAFT
11. FEED CHUTE
12. TRANSFER UNIT
13. SCAVENGING HOSE
14. EXIT UNIT
15. GUN INDEXING PIN
16. GUN DRIVE UNIT
17. CONTROL VALVE
18. TORQUE TUBE
19. GUN-MOUNTED GEARBOX

In the F-105D/F, a belted ammunition system was used for the M61A1 cannon. M50 high explosive incendiary (HEI) rounds were usually loaded, with one armor-piercing incendiary bullet to every six HEI rounds. In the previous F-105B system, conventionally linked rounds tended to break their links and jam the gun. For the F-105D/F, rounds were automatically fed, one at a time, into the six sliding bolts of the gun by a transfer unit located above the rear of the M61A1. Each of the six barrels could deliver 1,000 rounds per minute, and the system generally worked reliably. (USAF)

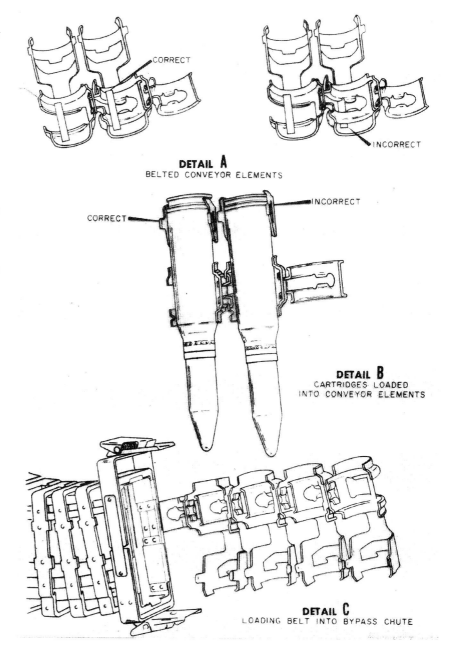

DETAIL A
BELTED CONVEYOR ELEMENTS

DETAIL B
CARTRIDGES LOADED
INTO CONVEYOR ELEMENTS

DETAIL C
LOADING BELT INTO BYPASS CHUTE

The complex process of setting and re-setting the small, hard-to-reach armament switches from "bombs" to "guns" to "rockets" or other ordnance was a problem in the heat of battle, and many firing opportunities were lost when pilots were unable to reset from "bombs" to "guns" as they came off a bombing run and immediately had to face enemy fighters. F-105F pilot Maj William Robinson was one of several aviators who accidentally selected "rockets" instead of "guns," thereby losing a MiG kill opportunity despite firing 460 rounds at a MiG-17. However, using a gunsight in air-to-ground mode did not prevent 333rd TFS/355th TFW pilot 1Lt Fred Wilson from shooting down a silver MiG-17 on September 21, 1966. His flight leader, Maj John Brown, might well have entered a claim for it if his gun had not jammed after 154 rounds, some of which damaged the MiG.

Criticism was also leveled at the lack of tracer rounds in the ammunition supply and the hazy images provided by the gun camera.

MiG-17

The MiG-17 was essentially a point-defense interceptor or an escort fighter with a 402-nautical-mile combat radius at 29,370ft in VVS service. It had a larger section of unswept, inboard trailing edge than the MiG-15, more rounded wingtips and two extra boundary layer wing fences. The wing, with a different airfoil, was stiffened and simple Fowler-type hydraulic flaps were included, lowered at 20 degrees for take-off and 60 degrees for landing. The main undercarriage units retracted inwards hydraulically into the wing root. A pneumatic system operated the main wheel brakes, charged the guns and provided cockpit pressurization.

Removing spent 20mm ammunition debris and replenishing the ammunition drum took a four-man team with an MHU-12A/M trailer, a powered loader (upper right) and an elaborate rig and winch arrangement – not visible here – to lower a filled drum into place from above a maintenance platform. (USAF)

The forward fuselage resembled the MiG-15's, with a pressurized cockpit, avionics and weapons bays, a gun camera and a circular air intake with a single vertical splitter diverting air around the cockpit section. A heavy-duty windscreen was flanked by Perspex sidelights and the cockpit was enclosed in a bubble canopy incorporating a TS-27 rearward-looking periscope. The SM-2 ejection seat was an improved version of the MiG-15's, useable above 800ft and featuring a retractable visor and additional anti-tumbling surfaces. The castoring nose undercarriage, with a single 19in. wheel, retracted forwards. Lowering the undercarriage required the pilot to activate a pump and allow pressure to build up, and then push the undercarriage lever to lower and lock the wheels.

A new rear fuselage section, detachable like the MiG-15's, was three feet longer, with a larger vertical tail and two-section rudder, a ventral fin and a horizontal tail swept at 45 degrees, with manually controlled elevators. The MiG-15 control system was retained, with powered ailerons and mechanical actuation through push–pull control rods. Two sideways-extending airbrakes, enlarged on later-production aircraft, were installed on the rear fuselage. Two rubber cells behind the cockpit contained 310.64 Imperial gallons (one of the two drop tanks beneath the wings of an F-105 held 450 gallons), and two 88-gallon drop tanks, or 132-gallon slipper tanks, could be attached beneath the wings.

VPAF technical personnel work on a MiG-17's Klimov VK-1 engine. The latter, reverse-engineered from the Rolls-Royce Nene (25 examples of which, and associated blueprints, had been donated to the USSR by the British government in 1946), was a single-spool turbojet with a centrifugal compressor. The entire rear fuselage could be pulled off the MiG-17, thus providing easy access to the engine and its accessories. (István Toperczer)

Early MiG-17s had a 5,952lbs thrust non-afterburning Klimov VK-1 or VK-1A turbojet (developing 6,040lbs thrust) using a single-stage centrifugal compressor and a single-stage turbine. It was accessible for servicing when the rear fuselage was removed at Frame 13. Later MiG-17F/PF and PFU models had an afterburning VK-1F engine including a convergent-divergent nozzle and an extended jet-pipe, providing 1,411lbs more thrust.

Although the overall power was barely a quarter of the F-105's maximum thrust of 26,500lbs, the early MiG-17's empty weight was only 8,373lbs, compared with 27,500lbs for an empty F-105D. Figures for maximum take-off weight contrasted even more strongly – 13,386lbs for a MiG-17 compared with the 52,838lbs of a fully loaded F-105D, emphasizing the design differences between a lightweight, cheap-to-build day fighter and a complex, long-range nuclear strike aircraft. Despite its light structure, stressed to 8g without external stores, the MiG-17 carried heavy gun armament.

The VPAF received 28 radar-equipped MiG-17PF "Fresco-Ds" in 1965 and used them primarily for nightfighting – Lam Van Lich claimed the VPAF's first nocturnal kills in the form of two A-1 Skyraiders (unconfirmed by US sources) on February 3, 1966. The antennas for the RP-5 search and track radar system are visible on the nose of Bort 4726 of the 921st FR shortly after its delivery from the USSR. (István Toperczer)

The earliest examples of the communist fighter delivered to the VPAF for training and operations were MiG-17 "Fresco-As" with non-afterburning VK-1A engines. They were followed from 1964 by around 70 MiG-17F "Fresco-Cs," starting with virtually identical Chinese-produced Shenyang J-5s. Soviet production had begun in 1952, and later batches came from that source rather than from China.

Afterburning VK-1F engines were installed, and although tests showed that they offered only marginal speed increases in level flight (around 30mph at 16,000ft),

vertical maneuverability was improved and service ceiling increased by 1,000ft. The VK-1F also had the advantage of leaving a minimal smoke trail, unlike most US engines, but afterburner light-up took more than five seconds (the F-105's took three to five seconds) and it could only be used continuously for around three minutes to avoid over-heating, or little more than 15 seconds in inverted flight. As the aircraft approached Mach 1 in level flight in afterburner it tended to climb, despite full-forward control column movement by the pilot. Like most early turbojets, acceleration was sluggish with the VK-1F, which took 15 seconds to reach full power from the idle setting.

The VPAF also received a modest quantity of MiG-17PFs, which were the first operational radar-equipped interceptors produced by the Soviet Union. The aircraft had an Izumrud-1 S-band air-to-air radar installed in a slightly longer nose, the search radar being housed in the extended upper intake lip and the tracking radar enclosed in a fairing attached to the air intake splitter. To maintain center of gravity, the heavy N-37D cannon was replaced by a third NR-23. Twenty-eight MiG-17PFs were supplied to the VPAF at the end of 1965, fitted with Izumrud-2 "Scan Rod" (RP-5) radar. Basically a copy of the MiG-17PF, the Chengdu J-5A (F-5A) was manufactured from 1965 until 1959.

The Nudel'man N-37D 37mm cannon that was the heaviest caliber of weapon installed in the MiG-17A/F was designed during World War II as a replacement for the Nudel'man-Suranov NS-37. Entering service in 1946, the "autocannon" as installed in the MiG-17 weighed 227lbs, of which its 40 rounds of ammunition

MiG-17F CANNON

The MiG-17's armament was essentially carried over from the MiG-15, providing a brief but heavy punch. A single 37mm Nudel'man N-37D gun, with 40 rounds, fired massive 26.5oz projectiles at a rate of 400 shells per minute with a muzzle velocity of 2,263ft/sec. A single hit could cripple an enemy fighter, but excessive recoil made the weapon hard to aim and gun gases could cause engine surges. Two Nudel'man-Richter NR-23 (Norinco Type 23 in Chinese J-5 aircraft) cannon were paired on the starboard side. This short-recoil 23mm gun fired up to 650 rounds per minute at the same muzzle velocity as the N-37D, and its projectiles (80 per gun) weighed 7oz each.

accounted for 66.25lbs. A single well-placed hit from an N-37D's 1.65lb shell could be devastating. At its slow 400 rounds-per-minute rate of fire, the shells could be seen as individual fireballs emerging from the gun muzzle.

From mid-1967, MiG-17 pilots often used head-on attacks on F-105s as they pulled up from a bombing run as a way of concentrating their gunfire, as the N-37D otherwise tended to scatter the shells due to control instability. F-105 pilots had the opposite problem in that their extremely accurate M61 gun combined with the aircraft's stability to focus its bullets on one "all or nothing" area as small as 15ft^2 even at a range of 3,000ft.

The MiG-17's two Nudel'man-Rikhter NR-23 23mm cannon, each with 80 rounds of ammunition firing at 650 rounds per minute, weighed 243lbs. The combined weight of fire including the N-37D was an impressive 35lbs per second, but the guns often lacked accuracy due to a primitive, bulky ASP-4NM gunsight that had difficulty in keeping a turning target in the frame. Furthermore, it was disturbed by considerable vibration when the weapons were fired. Visibility through the 2.5in. thick, bullet-proof windscreen was also poor. Although the guns were nominally effective up to a range of 3,500ft, pilots were advised to close well within 1,000 yards (3,000ft) before firing. For F-105 pilots, their K-19 gunsight was usually set for a range of 1,500ft.

THE STRATEGIC SITUATION

Although Cold War F-105 pilots would have expected to meet numerous MiG-17s over Warsaw Pact territory should a conflict have ever broken out in Europe, it was generally assumed that they would outrun them. Faster, missile-armed interceptors like the MiG-21 entered production in 1959, together with the Sukhoi Su-9s and Yakovlev Yak-28Ps, but TAC pilots' main concerns were SAMs and AAA, or being consumed by their own multiple nuclear detonations.

F-105s were among the first US tactical aircraft to visit the area that would become embroiled in the Vietnam War, although 18th TFW RF-101 Voodoos had been flying

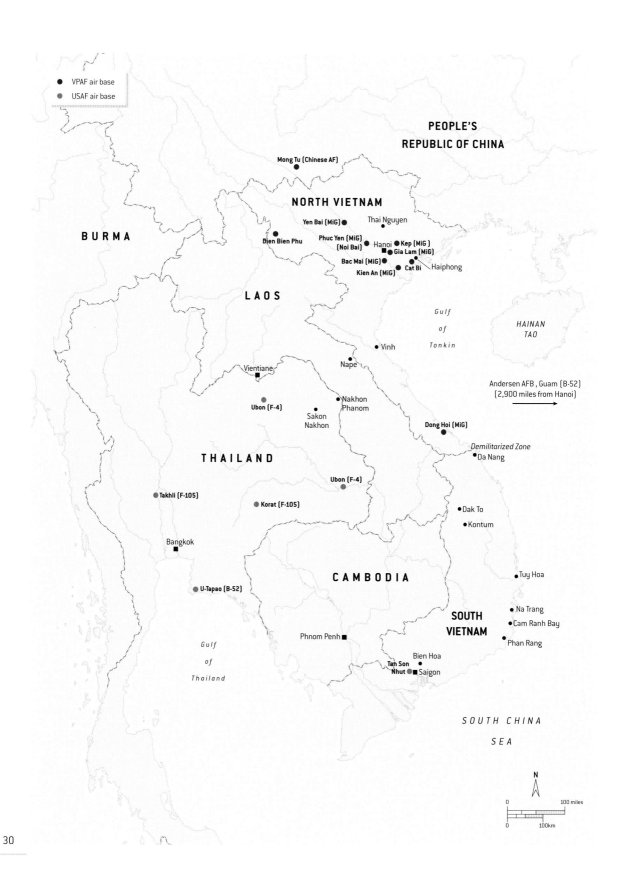

VPAF air base
USAF air base

PEOPLE'S
REPUBLIC OF CHINA

BURMA

Mong Tu (Chinese AF)

NORTH VIETNAM

Yen Bai (MiG)   Thai Nguyen

Phuc Yen (MiG)
(Noi Bai)   Hanoi   Kep (MiG)
Dien Bien Phu   Gia Lam (MiG)
                    Bac Mai (MiG)   Cat Bi
                    Kien An (MiG)   Haiphong

LAOS

                                        Gulf
                                         of
                                      Tonkin   HAINAN
                                                     TAO

                    Vinh

        Vientiane   Nape

                                        Andersen AFB , Guam (B-52)
                                        (2,900 miles from Hanoi)

        Ubon (F-4)   →

              Sakon   Nakhon
              Nakhon   Phanom

                                        Dong Hoi (MiG)

THAILAND   Demilitarized Zone
                                             Da Nang

                    Ubon (F-4)

Takhli (F-105)   Dak To

        Korat (F-105)   Kontum

Bangkok

                                        Tuy Hoa

CAMBODIA   Na Trang

U-Tapao (B-52)   Cam Ranh Bay

                                        SOUTH   Phan Rang
                                        VIETNAM

        Phnom Penh
                                        Bien Hoa
                        Tan Son
                        Nhut   Saigon

Gulf
of
Thailand

                                        SOUTH CHINA

                                             SEA

                                                N

                                        0   100 miles

                                        0   100km

30

covert missions over Laos from Don Muang RTAFB, near Bangkok, since October 1961 at the request of a neutralist Laotian government threatened by a communist insurgency. Their operations, code-named *Yankee Team* from May 22, 1964, soon involved F-105s to escort the RF-101Cs and attack any AAA sites that threatened this reconnaissance effort.

Two tactical fighter wings, the 18th at Kadena AB, Okinawa, and the 8th at Itazuke AB, Japan, converted to F-105Ds in 1962–63 as part of the "Flying Fish" program. In 1964 their mission was still nuclear alert, but the 18th TFW also introduced the F-105 to Thailand, where it would spend ten years in combat. The 44th TFS sent aircraft to Korat RTAFB in April 1964 for a peacetime exercise, *Air Boon Choo*, and returned in December as the first 18th TFW F-105 unit in combat. Six aircraft also went to Da Nang as Det 2 18th TFW in response to increasing Pathet Lao incursions in northern Laos.

US policy then favored the stabilization of Laos at a time when North Vietnam was already sending troops and supplies through this country to support Viet Cong opposition to the South Vietnamese regime and Pathet Lao aggression within Laos.

Washington's minimal application of air power in the early 1960s (a "measured and limited air action" in President Lyndon B. Johnson's words) did nothing either to deter the communist forces' ambitions or to wrest an agreement from Hanoi, after 11 years of negotiations, to sign a peace treaty preserving South Vietnam's independence. The 1954 Geneva Agreements had left Vietnam unsatisfactorily divided into communist North and non-communist South, and charged the USA with ensuring the South could defend itself.

A weak Saigon government, which was overthrown in November 1963, widespread corruption and increasing covert interference by North Vietnam made that task almost impossible from the outset, but it would be 14 years before the US government finally decided that the political cost of the attempt was too great. Its hesitation in using its overwhelming air power against North Vietnam was also based on fears that Hanoi's sponsors, the Soviet Union and China, would intervene and generate a major international conflict over a country which, for many Americans at the time, had little significance.

Hanoi was aware that tactical strike aircraft, mainly F-105s, could be quickly deployed from Japan. The US Navy's Seventh Fleet was on station in the Gulf of Tonkin with around 200 carrier-borne aircraft, and at a greater distance B-52s were on call from Guam. In the Pentagon, Chief of Staff of the Air Force Gen Curtis LeMay was vociferously advocating heavy preemptive bombing of North Vietnam. However, Viet Cong gains and declining political unity in South Vietnam persuaded Hanoi to respond to South Vietnamese attacks on radar installations near Vinh by attacking the US Navy intelligence-gathering destroyer USS *Maddox* (DD-731), triggering the Tonkin Gulf Incident on August 2, 1964. An unproven second attack on the ship initiated retaliatory US Navy *Pierce Arrow* air strikes on North Vietnamese naval assets.

With Congressional support generated by Hanoi's action, President Johnson deployed USAF tactical aircraft to bases in South Vietnam and Thailand. On August 12 the 36th TFS at Yokota AB – detached from the 8th TFW to the 6441st TFW, 41st Air Division (AD) – sent its second rotational batch of 18 F-105s

A flight of 921st FR MiG-17Fs taxi out for take-off at Noi Bai during the summer of 1965. Three of the four aircraft display colored fin tips to identify them to VPAF forward ground observers. "Red 2137" at the extreme left later served with the 923rd FR at Kep in 1966. (István Toperczer)

to Korat RTAFB led by 36th TFS commander Lt Col Don McCance.

Their first combat mission was flown on August 14 to provide cover for what proved to be a false alarm over a supposedly downed pilot. Called in to attack local AAA sites instead, they took some heavy ground-fire as they dived in, firing exploratory cannon bursts to try and locate the flak batteries. 1Lt Dave Graben, flying as wingman to Capt Jack Stressing, saw 37mm "red golf balls" heading for his F-105D and felt a hit in the rear of the aircraft. He cleaned off his stores and heard from his flight leader about large holes below the tail of the jet and a massive gash in the left tailplane. He flew the aircraft back to Korat for a perfect landing, proving the Thunderchief's toughness.

In response to increased US air activity, the first of 30 MiG-17 "Fresco-As" and the newly trained pilots of the VPAF's 921st FR flew from their Chinese base at Mong Tu to the newly completed Noi Bai (Phuc Yen) air base near Hanoi on August 6. Thirty pilots from Soviet training bases followed in the summer of 1965. As further proof of Hanoi's intransigence, Viet Cong guerrillas launched a surprise mortar attack inside the USAF base at Bien Hoa on November 1, 1964, hardening the US Joint Chiefs of Staff's determination to respond with B-52 strikes on Noi Bai air base. Secretary of Defense Robert S. McNamara and other civilian advisors persuaded President Johnson (two days away from a Presidential election) to forego such an attack, however. In that month, US tactical jet losses began with an F-100 and an RF-101C shot down over Laos.

Air activity was limited to a small number of attacks in the *Barrel Roll* and *Steel Tiger* campaigns of strikes on supplies and troops en route to South Vietnam – when they could be found. Da Nang-based F-105s flew their first *Barrel Roll* mission on December 14, 1964, with six F-105s led by two "pathfinder" RF-101Cs and covered by two flights of F-100 Super Sabres.

The 44th TFS's opening mission was on Christmas Day 1964 following an attack on the US-frequented Brink Hotel in Saigon. The F-105s struck a barracks at Tchepone (Xépôn) on one of the main Laotian supply corridors of the Ho Chi Minh Trail network. Lt Col William Craig, 44th TFS commander, led four F-105Ds in a somewhat inaccurate dive-bombing attack. Another *Barrel Roll* mission on January 13, 1965 by 16 44th and 67th TFS Thunderchiefs and eight F-100Ds cut a bridge at Ban Ken, in Laos, but Capt Al Vollmer's F-105D (62-4296) was shot down – the first Thunderchief loss over enemy territory.

Gen LeMay, incensed at what he saw as a weak US response, insisted that "we should go north. Our present strategies aren't working." Instead of "playing a losing game," he and other Joint Chiefs of Staff members advocated decisive, heavy attacks on North Vietnam to force a settlement. McNamara and Johnson's Special Assistant for National Security, McGeorge Bundy, also advised the president that current policies were ineffective, although Johnson still insisted on seeking peaceful solutions. However, after Viet Cong attacks on American troop installations at Pleiku, he was obliged to launch a retaliatory airstrike, Operation *Flaming Dart I*. Further Viet Cong action against US Army barracks at Qui Nhon triggered *Flaming Dart II* four days later.

Most of this operation's sorties against North Vietnamese Army (NVA) bases were flown by US Navy aircraft supported by Vietnamese Air Force (VNAF) A-1 Skyraiders, while the USAF contributed F-100s. They encountered no opposition from the fledgling VPAF, whose 35 MiG-17 and MiG-15UTI (trainers) at its only jet-capable airfield, Noi Bai, were supported by about 90 Soviet transports, helicopters and light aircraft. The 921st FR was not yet ready to openly challenge US air power.

Gen Joseph H. Moore, commanding the USAF's 2nd AD and its 166 combat aircraft (including 36 F-105s) from Tan Son Nhut AB, recommended Noi Bai as a priority target. However, US strategists were concerned that China could easily reinforce the fighter component from its own 300 frontline combat aircraft. Airfield attacks were ruled out unless VPAF or Chinese fighters openly resisted the USAF/ VNAF attacks that were being planned in February 1965 in an eight-week program following the *Flaming Dart* missions. Various target lists were drawn up, with the overall emphasis being on cutting off military supplies to North Vietnamese-sponsored forces in the South, initially by bombing railway bridges and marshaling yards south of the city of Vinh.

Meanwhile, President Johnson's emphasis was still on negotiation, and he feard that "a weak government in Saigon would have difficulty surviving the pressures that might be exerted against the south if we bombed the north."

A program of reconnaissance flights by US aircraft revealed that Hanoi was rapidly building up its anti-aircraft defenses, with 161 active AAA sites, many with SON-9A fire-control radars, around main routes, bridges and close to the Hanoi/Haiphong urban areas. While the *Flaming Dart* attacks were in progress, plans were made to send another 15 USAF combat squadrons to the area to augment the 13 that were already in place. The planned total included two F-105 squadrons at Korat RTAFB, two at Osan AB in Korea, four at Kadena AB, three at Yokota AB and one at Da Nang AB. The Japanese-based units would be in place to detach flights of F-105s to Thailand or South Vietnam as required.

There were numerous small airfields, inherited from French occupation, in North Vietnam, and the VPAF's first jet airfield (Noi Bai) was constructed with Chinese expertise between May 1960 and 1965, with sufficient facilities in place to accommodate the first MiG-17s by August 1964. The construction or modernization of six other airfields was ordered in mid-1965, including Kep, which was to house the second MiG-17 unit, the 923rd FR, with two squadrons of MiG-17A/Fs and four MiG-15UTIs from September 1965. Its eight-month construction period required the removal of several small hills to build its 7,200ft runway.

By February 18, 1965 President Johnson felt that the South Vietnamese government and military leadership was sufficiently stable to allow more

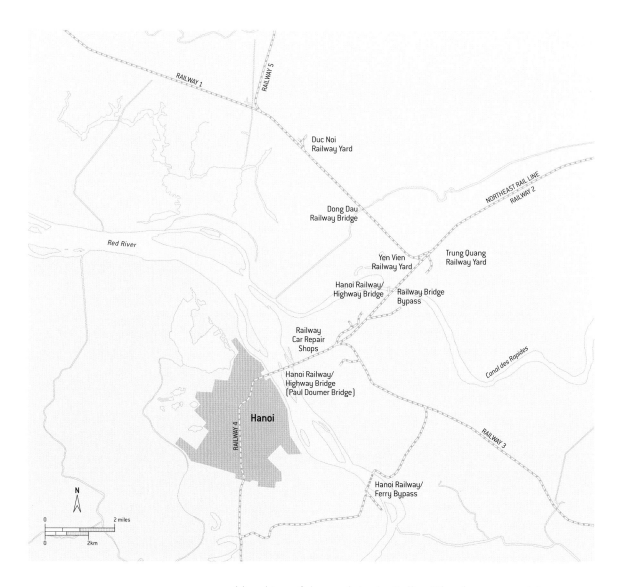

Railway and bridge targets for
F-105s in the Hanoi area during
Operation *Rolling Thunder*.

concentrated bombing of the north in the *Rolling Thunder* program. Management and targeting of this stop–start series of attacks was conducted mainly from the White House by Johnson, McNamara, Bundy and Secretary of State Dean Rusk through a complex, inefficient chain of command rather than by experienced military leaders. The Joint Chiefs of Staff list of 94 high-value targets was shelved and many were not hit until much later in the war after many unnecessary aircraft losses. The White House policy was based on gradual movement north towards Hanoi, with the Johnson administration hoping that the North Vietnamese leadership had capitulated before the capital was targeted.

The first *Rolling Thunder* strike was planned for 20 February, using US Navy aircraft with support from the VNAF and USAF. It had to be abandoned, however, when the Johnson administration received word of another potential Saigon government coup. Some political stability had been achieved by February 26, so, after several more strike postponements – two due to poor weather – *Rolling*

Thunder V was finally launched on March 2 against a backdrop of reports that more than 37,000 Viet Cong troops and their supporters had by then infiltrated South Vietnam.

Hanoi's resolution was further emphasized by its acceptance of the potential destruction of large parts of its country by bombing. Orders were issued to evacuate 50,000 civilians from the cities. *Rolling Thunder V* hit only two targets – Xom Bang ammunition storage area and barracks near the demilitarized zone (DMZ) and a naval base at Quang Khe. The Xom Bang strike force was the first to use only USAF tactical aircraft. Twenty-five F-105 bombers of the 18th TFW's 12th and 67th TFSs, armed with 500lb GP bombs, and 16 more as flak suppressors were joined by 20 B-57s and eight F-100s, with Super Sabres undertaking MiGCAP and ResCAP (covering possible rescue of downed crews) flights.

The target was destroyed, but so were five USAF aircraft, including three 67th TFS F-105D flak suppressors, hit while attacking AAA sites. In two cases pilots were making a second pass at the guns – a practice that was to cost Thunderchief units dearly during *Rolling Thunder*. Capts Robert Baird and K. L. Spagnola and Maj George Panas were all rescued, with Baird becoming subject of a combat rescue from North Vietnam. Spagnola and Panas coaxed their damaged Thunderchiefs over the border into South Vietnamese airspace before ejecting. 1Lt Hayden Lockhart, flying a 613th TFS F-100D, became the first member of the USAF to be captured in North Vietnam after evading the enemy for a week.

Although the mission was the first of many similar strikes, its outcome for F-105 crews, who were to fly three-quarters of the *Rolling Thunder* attacks, were to be repeated with tragic frequency.

The 562nd TFS/23rd TFW, whose aircraft were marked with blue-and-white tail bands, was another early visitor to Takhli RTAFB. It relieved the 563rd TFS, which had been in-theater since April 6, 1965 as the first USAF unit to complete a four-month combat tour since 1953. In September 1965 the 562nd TFS flew 533 combat missions with 24 pilots, and its silver-painted F-105s had completed 1,740 sorties after three months. F-105D 61-0116, with a cluster of M117 bombs destined for a Laotian target, has 50 missions marked up just forward of the wing leading edge nose – a practice which was soon discontinued as the pressure of operations increased. (USAF)

THE COMBATANTS

F-105D 61-0132 *HANOI Special* of
the 34th TFS/388th TFW at Korat
RTAFB would become a MiG-17
killer for 1Lt David Waldrop on
August 23, 1967 when he shot
down Le Van Phong of the 923rd
FR. Carrying a typical load of
M117 bombs, an AIM-9B and an
AN/ALQ-71 ECM pod, this aircraft
was among several F-105Ds with
the strike camera mounted in the
nose beside the AN/APR-25/26
ECM antenna rather than behind
it so that it could be directed
forwards. (Terry Panopalis)

"THUD DRIVERS"

After its long-delayed entry into USAF service, the Thunderchief, in its all-weather
strike F-105D/F configuration, soon proved to be a capable weapon whose
performance attracted recruits. Its stability, unbeatable low-altitude speed and
impressive size were unprecedented for a fighter. As pilot Murray Denton recalled:

My first impression of the F-105 was how large it was and how roomy the cockpit seemed. Coming from the F-106 Delta Dart, I couldn't believe the long take-off roll. I remember the night flights with "three bags" of fuel and water injection for more thrust. We would use all 9,000ft of runway and milk the flaps up. It was a very stable platform, and the faster it flew the better it got. It operated well from sea level to 15,000ft, and in military power the jet would run faster than any other aircraft at low level – it just didn't turn much. It also had a great gun and was a very stable bomber that could take hits and come home.

Pilots for the F-105 squadrons came from a range of backgrounds. Many transitioned from F-100s, TAC's previous main nuclear striker, when their units converted to the Thunderchief. Others, like Capt Wayne C. Warner, who had long wished to fly fighters, came from very different aircraft – in his case, a combat tour on the C-130 Hercules. Some had a very long history of fighter operations. Col "Jack" Broughton, who became Vice Wing Commander of the 355th TFW and flew 102 combat missions in Vietnam, started his frontline career flying P-47 Thunderbolts in 1946, saw combat in F-80C Shooting Stars during the Korean War and completed squadron service on a total of 13 fighter types including the F-105. For many of the F-105 pilots who went to war, their recent background had been in nuclear alert situations in Pacific Air Forces or US Air Forces Europe (USAFE) squadrons in the F-105D's first few years of USAF service.

Laden down with survival gear and a backpack parachute, Col "Jack" Broughton, Vice Wing Commander of the 355th TFW, climbs into his F-105D 62-4338 *Alice's Joy* at Takhli RTAFB. A veteran of combat in Korea in the F-80C Shooting Star, Broughton flew 102 missions in Vietnam. (Author's collection)

Capt Bob "Spade" Cooley was another former Korean War pilot who had flown F-86 Sabres, F-84Fs and then F-100s. Moving to the F-105 in West Germany, he found that, "it had a lot more power [than the F-100]. Its mission was essentially the same as the Super Sabre, and I didn't have a lot of trouble going from one to the other. There was a constant flow of planes from Bitburg and Spangdahlem ABs [both in West Germany] to Wheelus AB, Libya. We just took our turn for nuclear and conventional training on the El Uotia practice bombing range, undertaking skip-bombing, dive-bombing and gunnery."

Apart from practice gunnery against a towed dart target, air-to-air combat was notably absent from the syllabus, but, as Bob pointed out, "Nothing was a fast as a 'Thud' once it got going. It was the world's fastest tricycle. It had no air-to-air role unless forced into it." The transfer of USAFE F-105 pilots to the war increased sharply in 1966 as losses at the two Thai bases mounted.

Meanwhile, Bill Hosmer was an 18th TFW pilot at Kadena AB. "Sitting alert with those two [B28] Y1 1.1 megaton bombs was an ominous situation for me. I was scheduled to strike Shanghai airport first, then another target. After that I was supposed to head east until I flamed out. Then I would eject and be picked up by a US Navy destroyer."

Although their nuclear attack expertise would have little application in Vietnam, USAFE pilots found that their experience of persistently bad weather in Europe was good preparation for Southeast Asian monsoon visibility. Capt Ben Fuller, with the 7th TFS at Spangdahlem, recalled, "Our normal training consisted of flying radar low-level navigation and simulated bombing of targets throughout France and West Germany. The mission profile was low-level to the target and then a climb out to

F-105D COCKPIT

1. Standby compass
2. AN/APR-36 homing and warning ECM receiver threat display controls
3. Reflector gunsight
4. AN/ALR-31 threat light display
5. AN/APR-36 azimuth indicator
6. Drag chute handle
7. Remote channel indicator
8. Standby altimeter
9. Vertical airspeed mach indicator
10. Attitude direction indicator
11. Vertical attitude velocity indicator
12. Ground speed and drift indicator
13. Standby airspeed indicator
14. Standby attitude indicator
15. Horizontal situation indicator
16. Pressure ratio gauge
17. Tachometer
18. Landing gear lever
19. Weapon selection switch
20. Bomb mode selector switch
21. Instrument selector switch
22. Clock
23. Exhaust gas temperature gauge
24. Oil pressure gauge
25. Caution light panel
26. Cockpit lighting
27. Landing gear position indicator
28. Bomb NAV switch
29. Antenna tilt indicator
30. Fuel flow indicator
31. Electric power supply panel
32. Bomb arming switch
33. Clearance plane indicator
34. Radar scope
35. Fuel quantity indicator
36. Fuel quantity selector switch
37. Hydraulic pressure gauge (PRI one)
38. Hydraulic pressure gauge (PRI two)
39. Hydraulic pressure gauge (utility)
40. Flap position indicator
41. Emergency landing gear extension handle
42. Rudder pedals
43. Emergency brake handle
44. Throttle control
45. Air refueling handle
46. Auxiliary special weapon release handle
47. Control column
48. Weapons control panel
49. Oxygen regulator control panel
50. Electric power supply control panel
51. Flap lever
52. R-14 radar control panel
53. Pilot's seat
54. Control transfer system panel
55. Flight controls panel
56. Command radio and AN/ARC-70 UHF short range radio control panel
57. R-14 radar control panel
58. Canopy lock lever
59. Circuit breaker panels
60. Fuel system control panel
61. Automatic Flight Control System panel
62. AN/APN-131 Doppler navigation radar control panel
63. Friend or Foe/Selective Identification Feature control panel
64. Auxiliary canopy jettison handle
65. AN/ARN-61 Instrument Landing Set control panel
66. Emergency pitch and roll control panel
67. AN/ARN-62 TACAN control panel
68. Interior lights control panel
69. Exterior lights control panel
70. SST-181 X-band transponder control box
71. KY-28 CIPHONY voice security control panel

altitude for an instrument approach and landing using GCA [ground-controlled approach] assistance. Due to European weather, almost all landings were under instrument conditions."

The low altitude target approaches would prove particularly useful in Vietnam. One of the first major F-105 actions in *Rolling Thunder*, the "Spring High" attacks on SAM sites on July 26, 1965, were flown by the 563rd TFS at altitudes as low as 20ft – below the detection envelope of all enemy radars.

Col Boyd Van Horn "arrived at Bitburg AB in late 1965 and was assigned to the 53rd TFS commanded by Sandy Vandenburg. My old ops officer, Jim Kasler, was there, along with a bunch of old friends from Turner AFB, Georgia. They all volunteered to go to Southeast Asia and most went to Takhli RTAFB." Maj Jim Kasler became operations officer for the 354th TFS at Takhli, and he organized some of *Rolling Thunder*'s most effective attacks before being shot down and taken prisoner on August 8, 1966. Kasler was the only member of the USAF to be awarded the Air Force Cross three times.

Bob Cooley, was serving with the 9th TFS at Spangdahlem when he received orders to relocate to Thailand. "We were all trained and current in all the weapons delivery techniques, so that's why they came to the USAFE bases for crews. There was no specific theater preparation until we got there. My first mission was only the second time I flew from Takhli." Among the transfers from USAFE F-105 bases to the two Thai-based Thunderchief wings were Col William Chairsell, who went on to command the 388th TFW at Korat in August 1966, and his successor as commander of the 49th TFW, Col John Giraudo, who took over the Takhli-based 355th TFW.

Luckily, although air-to-air combat was not considered a likely scenario for the F-105, many of the pilots who joined the first deployments to Southeast Asia had gained that experience during previous fighter tours. As Col Broughton explained, "Most of us 'old heads' in the 'Thud' business had a good grasp on aerial combat. I don't think air-to-air was ever considered irrelevant in training, at least not at our level. We didn't have many trainees join us during my time in Southeast Asia. We needed experienced guys to go North, and if we got a new guy we taught him all we could on-scene."

For many of the newer pilots, their air-to-air practice had to be with other F-105s, often on an informal basis. Few had experience of relevant similar air combat maneuvering (ACM) with aircraft like the F-86, which was a good MiG-17 simulator, and their knowledge of the VPAF's then primary fighter often came mainly from reading a translation of its flight manual.

Joining the 24 pilots of each squadron in Thailand were the much greater numbers of personnel who comprised the bulk of any fighter unit. Whereas pilots ("drivers" to the groundcrew) often displayed their names on the canopy rail of a "Thud" but actually flew any jet that was assigned to them that day, the crew chiefs and maintainers for each F-105 were dedicated to that aircraft only.

Trained at Amarillo AFB, Texas, in F-105 maintenance, many 18-year-old recruits joined classes of 15, one of which would graduate weekly and be sent to an F-105 base

Sgt Neil Byrd takes a brief break from working on the main avionics bay of a Takhli-based F-105 in 1970. He specialized in the aircraft's automatic flight control system, whose four pull-out modules are at the lower right of the bay. There was an auxiliary electronics compartment aft of this main bay and a forward electronics compartment in the nose, together with other sensitive avionics in other locations, making the F-105's systems very vulnerable to AAA or SAM shrapnel. (Neil Byrd)

in Japan, Germany or the Continental USA – Nellis AFB, Nevada; McConnell AFB, Kansas; or Seymour Johnson AFB, North Carolina. The "fixers" learned to use their Channel Lock pliers, Crescent wrenches and Phillips screwdrivers on the retired F-105B airframes supplied for training, but they could not anticipate the punishing schedules that would rule their lives in wartime.

In 1964 each operational squadron had a section of an Organizational Maintenance Squadron (OMS) attached to it, such as the 18th OMS Blue section that looked after the aircraft of the 44th TFS "Vampires." Yellow section cared for the 12th TFS "Dirty Dozen" and Red section tended the 67th TFS "Fighting Cocks." All three units were in turn part of the 18th TFW at Kadena.

Each F-105 had a crew chief to prepare it for a mission and a team of specialists on call to provide anything from fuel, to repairs and ordnance, although crew chiefs would supervise installation of a refurbished engine or tire changes – each about an hour's work. Overall charge went to a Line Chief who allotted Assistant Crew Chiefs wherever they were required. The most time-consuming parts of the F-105 for maintenance were its radar system and bombing computer. Groundcrew at the Thai bases worked 12-hour shifts ("six-'til-six") for 90 days before getting a three-day leave pass.

A crew chief managed the start-up and pre-flight routines. Having strapped in the pilot, he plugged a communications cord into a socket on the nose ready for engine start-up. Most of the switch settings in the cockpit were already done and the pilot had to set his clock and adjust the altimeter tape display to the correct setting and barometric pressure.

After a final check by pilot and crew chief, there would be a countdown to engine start, keyed to the pre-determined time, and the pilot pressed the "start" button. A cartridge start would release thick black smoke from the cordite and tar contents of the charge. As the engine wound up to "idle" the instruments came alive and hydraulic and oil pressure could be checked. Bleed-air powering the air turbine motor would then supply electrical power to the other instruments and the utility hydraulics that operated the undercarriage, brakes, steering, gun and other vital systems. Further checks could then be carried out by operating the refueling probe and receptacle, landing lights, pitot tube heater, external tank pressurization and flaps.

When taxi time arrived, the crew chief disconnected his audio link, pulled away the chocks and guided the F-105 out from its revetment into the correct position in the flight. Groundcrews at the Thai bases earned the heartfelt support of their pilots for keeping the aircraft flying in such demanding circumstances. Maj James Kasler often praised his Takhli crew for enabling him to fly 91 missions without a single abort, and with only one small problem with ordnance.

Before a mission, the Force Commander (one of the most experienced officers) met with the flight leaders and the leading *Wild Weasel* crew to establish their exact routes to

Maintenance at Thailand's F-105 bases continued into the night. Here, 44th TFS/388th TFW F-105D 60-0423 receives attention to its RHAW antenna, with fuel and 500lb bombs already loaded for the morning mission. Groundcrew spent at least two hours turning an aircraft around. If a different configuration was required late in the schedule the aircraft first had to be de-fueled and its ordnance removed. Uploading bombs took about 30 minutes, but the whole reconfiguring process could take three hours of exacting teamwork. If the gun had been used, black residue had to cleaned off the left side of the nose. Minor combat damage was temporarily covered over with Typhoon duct tape. (USAF)

and from the target. All pilots received maps, target photographs and a form showing distances, timing, turn-points and planned fuel consumption details. A separate "words card" showed relevant call-signs and radio frequencies for the support aircraft like tankers, times for take-off, engine start, time-on-target and names with tail numbers of the individual F-105s and pilots. There were also code words to communicate details of the success or failure of the attacks and the location of enemy defenses, so that there was no danger of those transmissions reaching the ears of the defenders. Briefing included a view of the target map and routes, details of known and numbered SAM sites that could be a threat and estimates of the likely opposition from MiGs and AAA.

In 1965 missions tended to include a descent to around 500ft at about 50 miles from the target, and at a predetermined initial point the flight would light afterburners and climb to 12,000ft to identify the target visually and roll in to attack at the planned speed and dive angle. Those parameters were determined using speed, altitude and dive angle, with depression settings on the bombsight "pipper" set manually in the traditional way, rather than with the aircraft's bombing computer.

For aircrew, the basic combat tour was a year or 100 missions, whichever came first. The mission total could be accomplished in six months during *Rolling Thunder*, but the end of that campaign in November 1968 prolonged most pilots' stays in Thailand. The 100 mission total was calculated by doubling the World War II limit of 50. After February 1, 1966 it did not include missions over South Vietnam or Laos, which were not considered "counters" towards the 100. Capts Don Totten and Ben Bowthorpe from the 334th TFS were the first two F-105 pilots to complete their 100.

Several pilots were victims of the "99th mission" syndrome, being shot down on their penultimate operation and, in some cases, killed in action. On April 23, 1966 Capt Robert Dyczkowski became one of that number. As "Oak 2" in F-105D 61-0157, nicknamed *Shirley Ann*, he was hit by AAA as he pulled up from the target and was not heard from again. His fellow 421st TFS pilot Maj Bernard Goss, leading a later flight, was also hit near the target and ejected from F-105D 61-0048. He was presumed to have been killed after landing on a steep hillside.

In August 1966 the majority of 421st TFS pilots at Korat each completed at least 20 "counters." Most newcomers to Korat or Takhli RTAFB during *Rolling Thunder* arrived from the Replacement Training Unit (RTU) at McConnell AFB, where the 23rd TFW had taken over the training of F-105 crews on January 1, 1966, continuing in that role until November 1970. Previously, the 4520th CCTW had provided Thunderchief training at Nellis AFB using the 4526th Combat Crew Training Squadron (CCTS) that was established in April 1960, and it continued with this task until January 1968. The wing began F-105D training in September 1960, adding the 4523rd CCTS to the program until early 1967. The 4th TFW at Seymour Johnson AFB also acted as an F-105 RTU in 1966, producing two classes of pilots.

Many of the combat tactics used in Vietnam were devised and developed at the Thai bases, with the 469th TFS at Korat, as the first F-105 unit to be assigned permanent change of station to Vietnam, being a leader in that process. Its pilots averaged 1,500 flying hours and around two years on the F-105 at the time of deployment, making them some of the most experienced and capable pilots on that aircraft. By mid-1966, however, many of the more experienced pilots had either been lost or completed their tours of duty.

Whereas most MiG pilots remained with their squadrons indefinitely throughout the war, F-105 wings could see three generations of pilots pass through their units within as many years, with a few returning for second tours. The supply of replacement pilots then came from the two F-105 wings at Yokota or Kadena, but increasingly from the US-based training squadrons.

MiG MEN

Half a century after fighting each other over North Vietnam, former US and VPAF pilots occasionally meet up as fellow fighter pilots, comparing tactics and sharing each other's cultures. In 1965 they were all dedicated and professional officers, but there were many differences between them, not least in their governments' attitudes to the growing conflict.

For the North Vietnamese, *Rolling Thunder* was just the latest chapter in a centuries-old struggle for nationhood and freedom from colonial rule. To them there was no question of negotiating a settlement with South Vietnam, which they regarded as part of their country. The prospect of military defeat or surrender was unacceptable as they fought on relentlessly. Many USAF pilots, however, felt that they were being sent to fight a war that their own government did not want to win.

In 1965, many F-105 pilots had several years' experience on the aircraft, often with USAFE where training conditions for low-altitude strike missions in poor weather prepared them partially for Southeast Asia monsoons. Some had known Korean War combat and a few had flown fighters in World War II. Many came from families with long military traditions. North Vietnamese pilots usually had a very different background.

Although Ho Chi Minh had established an army to fight the French colonial rulers in the late 1940s, its initial air component consisted of two light trainers in the form of a de Havilland Tiger Moth and a Morane-Saulnier MS.343. Further technical instruction was based on shot-down aircraft from the French *Armée de l'Air*. Although Vietnamese generals wanted an air force, efforts were confined to theoretical study of navigation, mechanics and airfield construction, and even these were abandoned when the French were driven out and the subsequent 1954 Geneva Agreement banned the creation of an air arm. This was circumvented, however, by arranging for pilot training in China.

Popular Western mythology later portrayed the first batch of VPAF pilots only as young men who had probably never driven a car, let alone flown a jet fighter. In fact, the NVA imposed strict selection procedures, requiring its first recruits to have good educational backgrounds (although many came directly from manual jobs with minimal educational opportunities) and physical fitness, as well as political soundness.

Eighty students went to China in February 1956, 50 for fighter training at Changchun and 30 to be trained on the Tupolev Tu-2 bomber, Lisunov Li-2 transport and Mil Mi-4 helicopter. For the fighter group, basic training was given on the piston-engined Yakovlev Yak-18 "Max" prior to graduating to the MiG-15UTI "Midget" two-seater for jet indoctrination in 1957. The full course took eight years to complete, including four years spent flying with the PLAAF.

JAMES H. KASLER

Born in South Bend, Indiana, on May 2, 1926, Kasler moved with his family to Birmingham, Alabama, at the age of eight, by which point he was already fascinated by the heroes of the past and by adventure and wargames. At 17 he was keen to become a pilot, so he took the aviation cadet examination, but World War II was nearing its end so he was not needed as a pilot. Offered the choice of becoming a gunner or navigator instead, Kasler chose the tail gunner course, training in B-24s and then serving on B-29s on Tinian Island. He flew a few missions over Iwo Jima and Japan before returning home and re-joining the aviation cadet program and qualifying as a pilot in 1951.

Kasler flew F-80s and F-84B/Cs, which he described as "horrible airplanes," and then the F-86A – he made a

Col James H. Kasler. (USAF)

supersonic dive in a Sabre that damaged the flying surfaces so much that the fighter had to be written off. Assigned to the F-86E-equipped 4th Fighter Interceptor Group at Kimpo during the Korean War, he became an ace on May 15, 1952 after shooting down his sixth MiG-15. Three of these aircraft, he later discovered, were flown by Soviet pilots. His combat experiences in Korea during the course of his 101 missions left him with great respect for the MiG, which could fly considerably higher than the F-86 and could therefore allow its pilot to choose whether or not to engage American fighters in combat.

Assigned to the USAF's Nellis-based Fighter Weapons School postwar, Kasler tested the first six F-100As ("the worst airplane I have ever flown") and contributed to its development into the successful F-100D. He converted to the F-105 and joined the 36th TFW at Bitburg, and was subsequently posted from there to the 354th TFS/355th TFW in February 1966 as operations officer – Kasler was one of the first three USAFE F-105 pilots to be sent to Southeast Asia.

He became the only member of the USAF to be awarded the Air Force Cross three times, including one for leading the petrol, oil and lubricants (POL) strike on August 8, 1966 that saw him shot down by ground fire while trying to locate and protect his wingman, 1Lt Fred Flom, who had ejected earlier in the mission (Kasler's 91st). He had received "hero" coverage in the American press during the Korean and early Vietnam wars (Kasler had been labeled "the hottest pilot" in Vietnam in an article published in *Time Magazine*'s August 1966 edition), which contributed to the consistently brutal treatment he subsequently received during his 2,401 days as a PoW in Hanoi.

James Kasler retired from the USAF with the rank of colonel in 1975. He passed away on April 24, 2014, aged 87.

For many students the classroom years involved basic education in mathematics and science that they, unlike their American counterparts, would have been denied at school. Inability to speak their instructors' language was a fundamental problem for both pilots training in China, the USSR and Czechoslovakia and NVA students who would later be taught to use SA-2 missiles and radar-directed AAA. Many found this and the scarcity of interpreters insuperable, and the failure rate was substantial.

Among the second class of 12 students on the 1959 Chinese course was Luu Huy Chao, who joined the 923rd FR and claimed nine US aircraft destroyed, including the F-105D of 333rd TFS pilot Capt David Allinson (whose loss was attributed to AAA by US sources), and retired as a senior colonel. Also present was Vo Van Man, who claimed six victories serving with the 921st and 923rd FRs before being shot down and killed by Maj Sam Bakke and Capt Bob Lambert of the 480th TFS/366th TFW in an F-4C. Man destroyed 1Lt Stephen Whitman's 354th TFS/355th TFW F-105D 59-1755 on July 19, 1966 over Noi Bai.

Tran Huyen from that group claimed three F-105Ds, and the man who would become the highest-scoring MiG-17 pilot of them all was also a class member in 1959–60 following his basic training with the 910th Air Training Regiment. Nguyen Van Bay stayed with the MiG-17 for all eight of his claimed kills up to April 29, 1967. Two were F-105Ds, with damage inflicted on a third, although all were attributed to AAA by the USAF. Le Hai, another pilot who flew the MiG-17 from 1965 until 1974, claimed seven US aircraft between April 1967 and March 1972 in Shenyang J-5s with the 923rd FR. His F-105D engagement occurred on April 28, 1967, but the only Thunderchief lost that day was 44th TFS/388th TFW aircraft 58-1151 flown by Capt Franklin Caras (who was killed), which was credited to MiG-21 pilot Dang Ngoc Ngu.

Another 30 students were sent to Krasnodar Flight Officers' School, a massive four-airfield complex near the Black Sea where communist bloc pilots were trained. VPAF recruits often trained with students from Cuba and Hungary, who had their own training squadrons. The instructors unsparingly required their pupils to learn Russian. Training courses were as demanding as those provided in China, with failure rates of 80 percent at times and a heavy emphasis placed upon political motivation. For the Vietnamese pilots, their personal commitment to protect their country from "outsiders" and to "liberate" South Vietnam was a vital factor in their progress.

After theory classes and sessions in a primitive simulator, students flew 100 hours of basic training on Yak-18s (replaced in 1966 by Czech Aero L-29 Delfin jet-powered

MiG-17F COCKPIT

1. ASP-4NM gunsight
2. Throttle
3. Push-to-talk radio control
4. Aileron trim control
5. Flap and airbrake levers
6. ARK-5 radio compass tuning panel
7. Emergency canopy jettison handle
8. Cartridge-fired KK-2 ejection seat
9. Ejection handles (both sides of seat)
10. Rudder pedals
11. Extendable control column with gun, speed-brake and ordnance/tank jettison buttons
12. Ordnance control panel
13. Emergency landing gear control
14. Canopy lock (right)
15. Canopy lock (left)
16. Windscreen de-mist and ventilation tube
17. Main pneumatic air pressure gauge
18. Main hydraulic pressure gauge
19. Aileron trim switches
20. Map/document holder
21. Bullet-proof windscreen (64mm thick)
22. Side-light transparency (8mm thick)
23. Canopy sealing hose, pressurised to 3 bars (42.8psi)
24. KUS-1200 airspeed indicator
25. VD-17 altimeter
26. RV-2 radio altimeter
27. AGI-1 artificial horizon
28. EUP-46 turn-and-bank indicator (electric)
29. MS-15 Mach meter
30. VAR-75 vertical speed indicator
31. Padded gunsight reticule adjusting knob
32. White stripe for positioning control column in spin recovery
33. Pneumatic brakes control "bicycle" lever
34. Electrical panel
35. Panel with controls for fire detection, fuel control and engine ignition
36. KES-857 fuel gauge
37. Landing gear select indicator
38. Flare select switch
39. Brake pressure gauge
40. ARK-5 Automatic Direction-Finding indicator
41. DGMK-3 gyro compass display
42. EMI-3P fuel and oil pressure/temperature indicators
43. TE-15 engine rpm indicator
44. TGZ-47 engine exhaust gas temperature gauge
45. EM-10M indicator
46. Gyro-compass "align to north" button
47. Pilot's oxygen indicator
48. Undercarriage control handle
49. Undercarriage position indicator
50. Flap switch
51. VA-340 volt/ampere indicator
52. Master electrical switch
53. Cockpit over-pressure indicator
54. Extra armament control panel (only present on some aircraft)

trainers) followed by around 150 hours at Kushchovskaya airfield on the hard-worked MiG-15UTIs and early MiG-17As – a difficult transition for many pilots. Smaller in stature and lighter than the Soviet pilots for whom the MiGs were designed, the North Vietnamese found the aircraft physically taxing to fly. They sometimes weighed less than the minimum required for their ejection seat safety parameters, while height issues reduced their levels of visibility from the cockpit, particularly in the MiG-21. Extra seat cushions were often needed for the non-adjustable ejection seats. Weather restricted flying from the Black Sea bases mostly to the summer months.

A later entrant to the Soviet MiG-17 classes in 1962, Nguyen Van Coc, re-trained on the MiG-21 in 1965 and went on to become the highest-scoring MiG killer, with seven of his nine claims agreed by both sides. Among them were three F-105Ds, with damage to two others, including one flown by Maj Al Lenski, which recovered to Udorn RTAFB after an "Atoll" missile hit during the same engagement in which Van Coc shot down 1Lt Bob Abbott's 354th TFS/355th TFW Thunderchief (59-1726) – the 355th lost three F-105s on this date (April 30, 1967).

Training focused on daytime air-to-air tactics, which, by contrast, were minimal in the USAF's contemporary training programs. Recruits learned basic Korean War-type dogfighting techniques and clear-weather interception as well as ground strafing. Also, in 1956, a civil aviation flying club was set up at Cat Bi, in North Vietnam, to form the covert nucleus of a military air force and establish its No. 1 Training School. At that time 12 students visited Czechoslovakia, where they were trained to fly the Zlin Z 226 Trener aircraft, six of which were provided by their communist ally, complete with Czech instructors, for use at Cat Bi.

In April 1959 they were joined by the first successful group of 13 fighter-qualified pilots from Changchun, who were keen to pass on their newly learned skills. China also donated three Aero Ae-45 twin-engined aircraft, which were used at Gia Lam (Hanoi airport) for training navigators and radio operators for multi-engined types, and eight Yak-18s for pilot training. By May 1959 a formal military structure was in place, with regiments for transport and training as well as the Air Force Training School. As no overtly military aircraft types were present, the Geneva Accords were apparently not breached.

Flying training within Vietnam began at Cat Bi in May 1959, and in the following year 52 pilots with basic training on the Yak-18 went to China to convert to the

The retaliatory American attacks on North Vietnamese targets prompted the transfer of 16 of the VPAF's MiG-17A – half of its original Soviet-supplied batch – from Mong Tu in China to Noi Bai on August 6, 1964. This aircraft was amongst those flown from China, and groundcrew from the 921st FR have immediately set about refueling it. The engine starter can also be seen behind the trailing edge of the fighter's left wing. (István Toperczer)

MiG-17. A further 31 pilots that had trained on the MiG-15 with the PLAAF went to Tianjin, in China, for MiG-17 conversion. They later transferred to Mong Tu, where they were closer to Vietnam in case they had to respond to an emergency at home. The Chinese bases continued to act as refuges throughout the war for pilots who were pursued by US fighters or had their bases in North Vietnam hit by US air strikes.

The first MiG-17 class graduated at the end of 1962 and returned home to share in the indigenous training program. These pilots would eventually fly 32 MiG-17s and four MiG-15UTIs supplied by the Soviet Union to establish the VPAF's first fighter regiment, the 921st "Sao Do" (Red Star) FR commanded by Lt Col Dao Dinh Luyen, on February 3, 1964. For the moment, the MiGs remained in China.

Thirty more trained pilots returned to Noi Bai, and aviators prepared for a transport squadron were diverted instead to fighters in response to the escalating US air campaign. A second MiG-17 unit, the 923rd "Yen The" FR was formed at the newly built Kep air base in September 1965, commanded by Maj Nguyen Phuc Trach. Eighteen more pilots arrived from the USSR in November 1966, with an additional 14 graduating from Cat Bi in January 1968.

During 1967 the VPAF's operational emphasis in terms of its fighter force shifted to the MiG-21 "Fishbed," examples of which had begun to arrive in North Vietnam in late 1965. Many of the better-qualified pilots duly flew both the MiG-17 and the MiG-21. They also manned the 35 Chinese-supplied MiG-19S (Shenyang J-6) supersonic fighters delivered in February 1969. Extra training on the radar-equipped MiG-21PFM was provided at Kushchovskaya when that type was issued to the VPAF as a nightfighter in 1968.

Almost all the VPAF's training aircraft would subsequently be destroyed during the *Linebacker II* attacks of 1972, although China soon provided replacements.

Once they were established at Noi Bai, the pilots of the 921st FR worked with their Soviet and Chinese advisors on developing tactics to employ against the more numerous and technically superior American warplanes. That planning depended on the integrated defense system that Soviet technicians established, based on Soviet city defenses and connected to a far-reaching early warning radar network.

The VPAF and Air Defense Force were merged into one command, with a communications net that was to prove more efficient on many occasions than the American command-and-control systems in-theater. Nevertheless, many mistakes also occurred, and pilots were often supplied with inaccurate or late guidance information from the "battle rooms," where the situation in the air was plotted on Battle of Britain-style map tables. Because pilots had to adhere so closely to their operators' instructions they were not allowed to use their own initiative if

Nguyen Phi Hung, Ho Van Quy, Luu Huy Chao and Hoang Van Ky walk to their fighters at Kep air base in early 1967. The black bar visible on the nose panel of "Red 2431" is the antenna for the SRD-1M radar range-finder. Future aces Hung Chao and Ky would claim five F-105s destroyed between them. (István Toperczer)

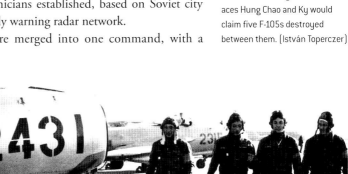

they suspected that they were being misdirected.

Sites for AAA batteries and (from mid-1965) SA-2 "Guideline" SAMs were all linked to a central GCI network that also involved the fighter force. For successful coordination of those elements strict control was required when it came to accurately timing the employment of SAMs, guns and MiGs against an American

North Korean MiG-17 "Doan Z" pilots rush out to the flightline at Kep to congratulate their returning brethren following a successful mission in 1967. The 80-plus volunteers that saw combat during the Vietnam conflict were required to wear North Vietnamese uniforms and flew alongside VPAF pilots during their two years in action. A number of them claimed F-105s shot down and, conversely, were killed in combat with the Republic fighter. (István Toperczer)

strike force. For MiG pilots, this meant that every aspect of their mission was tightly controlled from the ground and their natural fighter-pilot hunting instincts had to be suppressed. A few aviators who advocated ramming tactics against American "invaders" were also reminded of the scarcity of VPAF pilots and aircraft, although that desperate tactic would be revived during the massive B-52 onslaught on Hanoi in 1972.

The operational training process took around four months of intensive effort before the "Red Star" squadron was deemed ready to meet the "Yankee air pirates." However, their flying skills were still undeveloped in many cases, and losses occurred due to over-hasty decisions, inadequate formation-keeping with their flight leader or inability to control their aircraft successfully in a maneuvering fight. By the end of 1966 the radar and command systems were generally working efficiently, although errors did occur in the confined airspace around Hanoi resulting in several MiG pilots being shot down by their own AAA defenses. Le Trong Huyen, a MiG-17 flyer who claimed three F-105Ds after transitioning to the MiG-21, was one of those to fall victim to friendly fire.

In addition to the Soviet advisors who provided flying instruction and managed the maintenance of VPAF MiGs for several years, there were 70 highly trained and experienced North Korean People's Air Force (NKPAF) pilots known as "Doan Z" (Group Z) who flew both 923rd FR MiG-17s and 921st FR MiG-21s. Heavy losses of MiG-17s in late 1966 and early 1967 prompted North Korea's offer of assistance. The pilots served in VPAF units and dressed in North Vietnamese uniforms, but brought some of their own tactics to the battle. These included using a low-altitude pair of MiGs to draw away USAF or US Navy escort fighters and then climb to meet a second pair waiting to ambush the Americans at higher altitude.

From February 1967 the NKPAF pilots were commanded by Lt Col Kim Chang Xon, and they were supported by up to 800 North Korean groundcrew. Fourteen "Doan Z" pilots were known to have been shot down in MiG-17s, ten by F-105 pilots, although they were often known by North Vietnamese versions of their names to disguise their identities. North Korean pilots were also credited with a number of F-105s destroyed in return, and the last Thunderchief to fall to a MiG-17 was claimed by a "Doan Z" aviator on January 5, 1968 when the 357th TFS/355th TFW *Iron Hand* F-105F 63-8356 of Maj Jim Hartney and Capt Sam Fantle was gunned down. North Korean pilots claimed 26 American aircraft in total, many of which were disputed by US sources.

TRAN HANH

Born on November 28, 1932 to a poor family in Loc Vuong, Tran Hanh was one of the earliest recruits to the nascent VPAF in September 1949 when it was still the Air Force Research Committee, sanctioned by Ho Chi Minh and commanded by Ha Dong, at Huu Loc commune. His political credentials, including membership of the Youth Union in 1946 and the revolutionary movement from 1947, favored his selection for NVA membership in 1949, and he joined the Le Loi School for Officers the following year.

Like the other early Research Committee members, Hanh focused on studying the operations of the *Armée de l'Air* and basic aeronautical science, receiving instruction from a small number of defectors from that force who had decided to support the communist revolutionaries. When the Committee was disbanded towards the end of French colonial occupation Hanh continued his army career, becoming a political commissar for the 680th Battalion.

He had to wait until January 1956 for new opportunities to fly, however. Hanh's background made him an ideal recruit for pilot training in China that year, graduating to the MiG-17 as commander of the 2nd Company of the VPAF in 1960 and commander of the 1st Company of the newly established 921st FR in August 1964. When the squadron returned to Noi Bai on August 6, 1964, he and his wingman Nguyen Nhat Chieu were members of the first flight of MiG-17s to be placed on alert later the same day in case of US attacks.

Hanh quickly earned a reputation for being a skilled MiG-17 pilot and flight leader, with his achievements as a combat pilot first coming to the fore on April 4, 1965 – only the second day of the 921st FR's direct participation in combat. A US Navy F-8 had been damaged in a surprise attack by Pham Ngoc Lan's MiG-17 the previous day, and on the 4th Hanh led the second MiG flight into action. During the second attack by 18th and 355th TFW F-105s on the Ham Rong Bridge, Capt "Smitty" Harris's F-105D (62-4217) was brought down by AAA. Two more Thunderchief pilots who were orbiting to await their bombing runs due to timing problems, were fired on by MiG-17s and both pilots were killed. They were the first USAF aircraft to be destroyed by MiGs.

Hanh's flight had been vectored in for a hit-and-run attack, and he fired MiG-17 2618's three guns at

F-105D 59-1754 flown by Maj Frank Bennett, who ejected but was drowned. Tranh Hanh had to crash-land his own aircraft after losing contact with ground-control when he was pursued by US fighters. The second F-105D (59-1764), flown by Capt James Magnusson, fell to Le Minh Huan. The VPAF pilot was himself shot down and killed – possibly by an F-100D – shortly thereafter.

Hanh led a MiG-17 flight that claimed a USAF CH-3C search-and-rescue helicopter in November 1965, and he was one of four pilots who were honored in a ceremony in December 1966 – by then he had taken command of the 921st FR. He became Deputy Commander in Chief of the VPAF in March 1972 and overall commander in 1974, rising to Deputy Chief of Staff in 1976. After four years as Deputy Minister of Defense, Hanh retired as a Lieutenant General in 2000. His role in national politics remained strong throughout that time, exemplified by his membership of the Central Committee of the Communist Party of Vietnam in his final years of office.

Capt Tranh Hanh. (István Toperczer)

COMBAT

Some of the earliest MiG kills achieved by the USAF were credited to F-4C pilots undertaking MiGCAP flights for F-105 strikes. During the April 23, 1966 mission against the Bac Giang Bridge northeast of Hanoi, four flights of 388th TFW Thunderchiefs were greeted by unexpectedly heavy AAA. After a MiG warning, one of the 555th TFS/8th TFW Phantom II flights headed for the four incoming MiG-17s while the Thunderchiefs continued towards the target. "Dayton" F-4C flight detected the MiGs on radar at 15 miles and met them head-on, firing missiles without success.

Three agile MiGs soon managed to secure a firing position on "Dayton 02," but Capt Max Cameron and 1Lt Robert Evans in "Dayton 03" launched an AIM-9B that exploded in a MiG's tailpipe. Capt Robert Blake and 1Lt S. W. "Dub" George pursued another MiG-17 and destroyed it with an AIM-7 Sparrow, securing only the fifth MiG kill by a USAF F-4 crew over Vietnam.

Nevertheless, communist fighters still destroyed two F-105Ds from the 421st TFS, with the loss of Capt Robert Dyczkowski and Maj Bernard Goss (in 61-0048), and saw a chance to claim a third when they spotted a lone Thunderchief that had become separated from its flight in the last wave of attackers. Capt Carl Hicks was at the controls of the solitary F-105D, and he passed three MiG-17s on a reciprocal heading as he left the target. The MiGs reversed their course, caught up with him and fired several times, but Hicks escaped their attack by diving into the cloud-base and eventually re-joining his flight.

The following day, when the bridge was re-attacked, 469th TFS CO Lt Col William Earl Cooper lost his life when his F-105D (61-0051) was brought down by an SA-2. 1Lt Jerry Driscoll, "Pecan 4" in the second F-105 flight, was killed minutes later when his aircraft (62-4340) was hit hard by AAA during his bombing run.

The predictable policy of re-attacking heavily defended targets, using the same heavily defended approach routes, immediately after the first raid was a costly one for the F-105 squadrons whose M117 bombs were often insufficiently powerful to destroy the strongly constructed bridges around Hanoi. In the case of the Bac Giang Bridge, three further attacks were ordered in the final days of April but it remained open. The structure was finally knocked out on May 5 by two F-105 flights, each dropping two 3,000lb bombs. The deadly effects of Hanoi's predominantly AAA and SAM-based defenses were increasingly evident.

MiGs were absent from the two F-105 wings' largest attack of May 1966 – a joint assault on the Yen Bai munitions complex on the 10th. The target area, a railway marshaling yard with many storage buildings, required 25 flights of aircraft (including the recently arrived and very secret 13th TFS/388th TFW F-105F *Wild Weasel III-1* SAM suppressors) to knock it out. The Yen Bai mission also marked the F-105's first use of the CBU-24/B cluster bomb against AAA sites. Although numerous F-4C MiGCAP flights kept the VPAF at bay, two F-105Ds were lost to AAA.

Another major combined assault successfully took place on June 29–30 when the *Rolling Thunder* planners' attention turned to a

Ranking MiG-17 ace Nguyen Van Bay is seen here wearing his seven "Huy Hieu Bac Ho" ("Uncle Ho" badges). After each aerial victory officially recognised by the VPAF, pilots were awarded the "Huy Hieu Bac Ho." Three of the badges were for downed F-105Ds, although USAF records stated that all of these aircraft fell to AAA. (István Toperczer)

vital strategic target in the form of North Vietnam's POL storage facilities. Seven sites near Hanoi were attacked over two days by 32 F-105D/Fs, this operation being planned and led by Lt Col James Hopkins (469th TFS CO) from Korat and Maj Jim Kasler (354th TFS operations officer) for the Takhli force. The planning phase involved thorough examination of intelligence data on the defenses in the area, and it quickly became clear that up to 10,000 AAA weapons of 37mm caliber or above were poised to meet the attack, in addition to MiGs and SAMs.

On June 29, "Crab" flight, a Korat *Iron Hand* foursome, was intercepted by four MiG-17s as they approached the target along "Thud Ridge," having just shut down a SAM site with LAU-3A rocket pods and AGM-45 Shrike missiles. The MiGs were flown by Nguyen Van Bay, Phan Van Tuc, Vo Van Man and Tran Huyen. F-4C MiGCAPs were positioned to "sit" on the VPAF jet bases and deter other MiGs from taking off to intervene, but the lack of communist fighter activity puzzled Kasler, as did the small number of SAMs fired in the direction of the F-105s, one of which narrowly missed a 388th TFW aircraft.

The North Vietnamese appeared to have been taken by surprise, having not moved enough of their many guns into the immediate vicinity of the target. He did see two MiGs ready to take off from Noi Bai, which was "out of bounds" to American strike aircraft, as he passed it. Two more were engaged by two Korat pilots near Hanoi. They used afterburner to catch the MiG-17s, and both pilots fired at the VPAF fighters from 1,000ft without the help of their malfunctioning radar gunsights. The MiGs used their superior turning ability to avoid the 20mm shells, and the F-105s were forced to break away – a situation which would recur repeatedly in 1966–67.

"Crab 4" saw Bay's flight closing in and turned away with "Crab 3" (Maj Kenneth Frank), avoiding cannon rounds from Huyen and Man who had opened fire out of range but claimed damage to the canopy of one of the F-105s. Meanwhile, "Crab 1" (an F-105F flown by Maj Richard Westcott and Capt Herbert Friesen), flying one mile ahead of "Crab 3" and "4," saw the MiGs and engaged afterburner. Westcott banked

51

On June 29, 1966 – the day that Maj Fred L. Tracy claimed the first F-105 MiG kill – VPAF Nguyen Van Bay and Phan Van Tuc of the 923rd FR each claimed a Thunderchief destroyed. Only one was actually lost in that day's massive strikes, Maj Murphy Jones' 60-0460 reportedly being hit by 85mm AAA. However, Tuc's gun camera film was the VPAF's evidence that he was shot down by a MiG-17. This frame shows an F-105D, allegedly Jones', with both the air brakes and afterburner operating. Three other F-105Ds were damaged during the mission. (István Toperczer)

to the left and the MiG pilots saw him jettison his ordnance as Bay fired at "Crab 2," flown by 421st TFS CO Maj Fred L. Tracy. His F-105D (58-1156) was hit by nine 23mm and 37mm shells, one of which entered the cockpit without exploding and knocked Tracy's hand away from the throttle quadrant, abruptly shutting off the afterburner. It also wrecked his gunsight, oxygen controls and other cockpit instruments.

Despite this, Tracy performed a high-g barrel roll as Phan Van Tuc's MiG-17 overshot and flew into his "12 o'clock" position. Lacking a gunsight, Tracy aimed his cannon visually, using the nose-mounted pitot tube to give crude guidance, and sprayed the MiG with 200 rounds. He immediately observed many hits on its fuselage and wing root. "Crab 4" also fired at it but Tracy's bullets were the only ones seen to impact the MiG. As it flew into cloud, Tracy saw the fighter's wing begin to fold over the fuselage before he lost sight of it.

The fight continued, with Maj Frank firing at a MiG that had damaged "Crab 1's" tail surfaces with gunfire. Westcott also shot at two of the MiGs as they headed for Gia Lam airfield. The four F-105s then returned to Korat, leaving a pillar of smoke rising to 35,000ft from the burning oil tanks. Although the VPAF denied the loss (instead crediting three of its pilots, including Phan Van Tuc, with two F-105s destroyed), MiG-17 wreckage was reported later by intelligence sources and Tracy was eventually credited with the first MiG kill by an F-105 pilot. The only Thunderchief loss was in fact from the last flight over the target, with "Opal 2" (F-105D 60-0460 from the 333rd TFS/355th TFW, flown by Capt Murphy Jones – he became a PoW) being hit by 85mm AAA.

In a second POL attack near Hanoi on June 30, the 388th TFW F-105D (62-4224) of Capt Robin Nierste was hit by AAA, and he managed to coax it for 200 miles into Laos before the engine gave up. His jet duly became the 100th F-105 combat loss in Vietnam.

"Black Sunday," August 7, 1966, brought particularly heavy attrition. Eight US aircraft were lost during POL attacks as the North Vietnamese focused their defenses more effectively. Five of them were Thunderchiefs, with two 333rd TFS/355th TFW F-105Ds being the first to go down. Their pilots, Capt John Wendell and Maj Willard Gideon, became PoWs in Hanoi. Wendell's aircraft (ex-36th TFW F-105D 60-0499) was hit by an SA-2 during its bombing dive and Gideon's 61-0140, christened *The Lone Star Special*, took flak hits in the tail area and became uncontrollable.

Another Takhli aircraft, *Iron Hand* F-105F 63-8358 of the 354th TFS, was next to fall after firing at a SAM site and then being hit by an SA-2 that detonated the aircraft's 20mm ammunition drum. Fire eventually burned through the controls and Capts Ed Larson and Mike Gilroy ejected but were recovered by a USAF HU-16B amphibian. A second 354th TFS *Wild Weasel* F-105F (63-8361) flown by Capts Robert Sandvick and Thomas Pyle was hit by 85mm AAA while attacking a SAM site and both men became PoWs. Its loss left Takhli with only one operational *Wild Weasel* F-105F, and by August 17 five out of the eleven *Weasels* delivered to Southeast Asia had been destroyed during lethal *Iron Hand* missions.

The day's final loss was 1Lt Michael Brazleton in 357th TFS F-105D 62-4370, hit by 100mm AAA during its bombing run. Flying his 111th combat mission, he too

was taken prisoner. The attrition suffered on August 7 underlined the deadly efficiency of North Vietnam's SAM and AAA defenses, which were destroying far more US aircraft than the MiG squadrons.

July 1966 saw increasingly effective use of F-105F *Wild Weasels* and a growing realisation by the North Vietnamese of this threat to their SAMs. They began to target MiG-21 interceptions against the *Iron Hand* F-105 flights, believing that the faster "Fishbeds" had a better chance of penetrating the USAF fighter escort screen to launch stabbing attacks on the *Weasels* as they focused on the SAM sites.

A typical interception occurred on July 7 when "Opal" flight, led by Capt M. M. Angel, fired a Shrike at a "Fan Song" radar just as wingman Maj Robert Phillips saw a MiG turn inside the maneuvering F-105Fs and fire two "Atoll" missiles that were unable to match Capt Angel's turn. Phillips attempted to alter his complex armament switches so that he could jettison his two Shrikes and switch to "guns," but it was too difficult a task in the circumstances. Both pilots out-ran the MiGs at low altitude at 650 knots and escaped. They also found that their chances of retaliating against the MiGs were impeded by condensation on their cockpit canopies, which progressively blanked off all but the windscreen panels in the humid air at low altitude and high speed.

MIXED MiGs

Interceptions combining high-altitude slashing supersonic attacks by MiG-21s with low-altitude MiG-17 attacks were used increasingly in July. Four MiG-17s engaged two flights of F-105s during a July 19 mission and Thunderchief pilots claimed gunfire damage to three of them. A big POL attack by 16 F-105s that day gave Jim Kasler a chance to add to his tally of MiG kills from the Korean War, but he was denied his seventh victory by the performance inadequacies of the AIM-9B Sidewinder.

His leading flight had been pursued by three MiG-17s, which had forced the F-105 pilots to jettison their Mk 84 and M118 bombs (the primary intention of the MiG

Wild Weasel F-105Fs, leading the F-105D attack formations, came under increasing attack from VPAF fighters as 1966 progressed and the threat they posed to SA-2 sites grew. Armed with an AGM-45A/B Shrike anti-radiation missile under its right wing, which was usually counterbalanced by a drop tank under the other wing, 63-8277 heads northward on a mission in 1966. Maj John Dudash and Capt Alton Meyer of the 333rd TFS/388th TFW were shot down by a SAM in this aircraft during the attack on the Thai Nguyen thermal plant on April 26, 1967. (Jim Rotramel)

interceptions). They reversed to face their attackers, and the second element leader fired his cannon at a MiG-17, observing smoke and debris emerging from its wing. Kasler launched an AIM-9B at another MiG, but the missile's seeker head would not lock onto the target. His other Sidewinder also refused to guide, possibly because it was fired outside launch parameters.

Kasler then entered into a 20-minute maneuvering fight with a 923rd FR MiG-17 – the longest dogfight of the war to date. He used his afterburner, leading-edge flaps and long experience of fighter combat to stay out of the MiG's persistent gunfire, almost flying into the ground at one point as the turning fight inevitably forced them to lose altitude.

This frame from Nguyen Van Bien's MiG-17F gun camera (or that of Vo Van Man) allegedly shows 1Lt Steve Diamond's 354th TFS/355th TFW F-105D (60-5382) taking cannon-fire hits in its wing. Diamond did not survive the subsequent crash. (István Toperczer)

Two F-105Ds from the second strike flight briefly engaged the MiGs before losing sight of them. When the VPAF fighters finally broke away, probably low on fuel or ammunition, Kasler followed one back to its Noi Bai base. His jet was in turn fired at and damaged by Nguyen Van Bien's MiG-17. He was also surrounded by a heavy 37mm flak trap and had to head for home, knowing that MiGs on the ground at their own airfields could not be attacked at that time. The communist fighters still aloft were, in any case, diverted to Gia Lam to avoid the F-105s.

Kasler's wingman, 1Lt Steve Diamond (in 59-1755), attempted to shoot Bien's MiG off his leader's tail, closing to within 50ft of the fighter and scoring some hits on it before the pilot broke away in a 6g turn. Diamond was then shot down by future ace Vo Van Man and did not survive.

August 8 brought three more F-105D losses, including Maj Jim Kasler in 62-4343, consigning him to more than six years of imprisonment. Again, all three aircraft were victims of AAA, and the losses to the densely packed flak batteries continued four days later with two on a POL attack and three more on August 14 when more POL targets were hit around Thai Nguyen. The POL campaign was proving incredibly costly for the F-105 wings, and continued access to Haiphong harbor – which was still off limits for American bombers – meant that fuel supplies were quickly replaced by North Vietnam's allies.

The MiG-17 pilots remained very active in July and August 1966. Five made brief diving attacks on F-105 flights during a July 20 mission, which also saw MiG-21s approach a Thunderchief flight that jettisoned its drop tanks and went to "air-to-air" armament mode. The MiG flight may have mistaken the tanks for jettisoned bombs and broke away, leaving the F-105s to continue with their attacks.

The first encounter with MiG-17PFs occurred on July 22 when VPAF pilots salvoed unguided rockets at F-105s. One of the Thunderchief pilots returned fire, expending 100 rounds in a head-on attack on a MiG, although neither side scored hits. A camouflaged MiG-17 moved in behind a 355th TFW aircraft as the F-105 climbed off its target during another July mission, but the communist fighter broke away when its pilot saw the remaining two flight members closing in behind him. At that point future MiG killer Maj Fred Tolman, No. 3 in the flight, noticed another MiG-17 advancing on his tail. "They liked to keep one or two aircraft at medium altitude and another element at an extremely low altitude, but within sight of the high element. I'm sure that many of the MiGs were camouflaged on this day. They put two or three right down on the deck, which effectively hid them from view from an attacking pilot who would see the high element and go after them, allowing the low element to jump up behind the attacking aircraft."

A VPAF tactical review in July 1966 reinforced the advice to employ these tactics, and they were used again on August 17 to catch F-105s as they climbed away from their bomb deliveries. A Thunderchief flight-leader, pursued in that way, dived to such a low altitude that he had to pull up to cross the paddy field dikes in his path, while his wingman, without time to re-set his weapons switches from "bombs" to "guns," fired a few shells to distract the VPAF pilot. At Mach 1.2 on the deck, his leader escaped intact.

That same day, two flights of 923rd FR pilots (Le Quang Trung and Ngo Duc Mai from Noi Bai and Nguyen Van Bien and Phan Van Tuc from Gia Lam) were told to defend the Duong Bridge near Phu Lang Thuong and the area north of Noi Bai from attack by 16 F-105s. They converged on the Duong Bridge and intercepted "Honda" flight of F-105Fs from the 34th TFS/388th TFW that had become separated from the main force by weather but had nevertheless succeeded in attacking a SAM site with Shrikes. Two SA-2s were launched at "Honda" flight and one exploded between the leading F-105 element

A follow-up rocket attack was frustrated by the appearance of the MiG-17s on their tails. A burst of 23mm gunfire caused damage to "Honda 1's" wing and vertical stabilizer, probably leading to future ace Trung's claim for an F-105 destroyed. Maj William Robinson and Capt Peter Tsouprake, surprised to see a MiG in an area in which SA-2s provided the main defense, called in their wingman to get the MiG "off their ass."

Korean War veteran Maj Ken Blank, in F-105D 60-0458 as "Honda 2," cleaned off his ordnance and moved into a position 500ft behind the MiG, flown by Pham

OVERLEAF

On July 19, 1966, four F-105 flights from the Takhli-based 354th TFS/355th TFW targeted a POL storage site near Hanoi. The aircraft were supported by two F-4C MiGCAP flights and an EB-66 radar jammer, which had F-104C escort. Strike leader Maj James Kasler and his wingman 1Lt Steve Diamond (in F-105D 59-1755) were at 4,000ft heading towards their target, having already evaded four SAMs and AAA, when Diamond saw five MiG-17s near Noi Bai. Kasler's flight jettisoned their ordnance and he turned to fire at Nguyen Van Bien's leading 923rd FR MiG-17, which quickly turned behind him, starting a strenuous 15-minute dogfight. The MiGs subsequently made seven firing passes at him and Diamond. Bien's wingman Vo Van Man fired at Diamond, who in turn damaged Bien's MiG. Other F-105s intervened, driving off some MiGs, but Diamond's aircraft was fatally damaged by Man. Diamond ejected from his blazing Thunderchief as the biggest aerial conflict of the war to date continued. When Kasler himself was shot down on August 8, 1966, his captors stated that Diamond had died of a ruptured spleen. Man's MiG-17F "Red 2047" was later used by Nguyen Van Bay for his attack on the cruiser USS *Oklahoma City* (CL-91) on April 19, 1972.

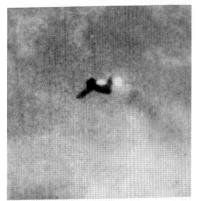

One of the MiG kills that was made without a gunsight was Maj Ken Blank's on August 18, 1966 as "Honda 02." Closing to within 500ft of Pham Thanh Chung's 923rd FR fighter, Korean War veteran Blank ignored the complex set-up procedure for a gun attack and fired 216 rounds using "eyeball computation" when the MiG filled the center of his windscreen. Chung was so preoccupied with shooting at "Honda" flight leader Maj Robbie Robinson, he had failed to spot Blank in his "six o'clock" position. (USAF)

Thanh Chung. Unable to set up his gunsight in time, he still fired 216 rounds and saw the MiG burst into flames and crash. An F-105 pilot in "Manila" flight who also saw the VPAF fighter hit the ground fired at a second MiG-17 without a gunsight but missed, after which the F-105s headed back to Korat. The only F-105F loss that day was 354th TFS *Wild Weasel* 63-8308, in which Majs Joseph Brand and Donald Singer were killed after it suffered AAA hits near Van Yen.

Five days prior to Blank's MiG-17 kill, the most intense dogfight since Kasler's July 19 engagement had occurred (on August 12) when Phan Van Tuc and Luu Huy Chao took off from Gia Lam to intercept an afternoon F-105 formation attacking the Thai Nguyen industrial complex. 1Lt Martin Neuens' 333rd TFS F-105D (62-4323) was shot down by AAA (but claimed by Chao) and another F-105D (61-0156) from the squadron was hit while strafing a target of opportunity on the return flight. Capt David Allinson ejected successfully but no contact was ever established with him.

His squadron set up a RESCAP orbit over the crash site, ready to cover for the arrival of a helicopter – a situation which often attracted MiGs. Tuc and Chao duly intervened and the F-105 pilots responded, firing more than 2,000 rounds at them and seeing damage inflicted on both MiG-17s. Inoperative Thunderchief gun cameras meant that no record was made of these hits, however, and there was no opportunity to use AIM-9Bs due to the close-in nature of the long-running dogfight.

From early September to the end of 1966 VPAF fighter activity increased markedly, with *Iron Hand* F-105D/Fs still being a primary target for MiG-21s. This led to almost daily sightings of "Fishbeds" and "Fresco-Cs." On September 9 an F-105F pilot was able to turn the tables on a MiG-21 interception and fire 600 rounds at the fighter's tail, but without visible hits. MiG-17s attacked another Korat F-105F flight five days later over the Dap Cau Bridge, intercepting the *Weasels* as they left the target and trying to draw them into an 85mm flak trap. The leading *Wild Weasel* pilot was able to gain a firing position on one of his opponents, only for a shear pin in his M61 gun to break after only six rounds had been fired.

In both cases the MiGs had been waiting at low altitude, below the "sight" of the EC-121 *Big Eye* airborne early warning and control aircraft that was undertaking a radar picket patrol offshore.

Three more flights of 388th TFW Thunderchiefs followed up, each with 3,000lbs of bombs. Their bridge target was within 15 miles of the airfields at both Noi Bai and Kep, making further MiG intervention almost inevitable. One pilot cleaned off his pylons and worked his way into a good firing position behind a MiG-17, although it then executed a typical sharp turn and escaped.

As the F-105 flight began to reform and egress, three more MiG-17s dived at them out of the low sun on the horizon, heading for Capt John Malone and 1Lt John Casper, Nos. 3 and 4 in the flight. Casper, from the 421st TFS, broke away and was hit by 57mm AAA as he crossed the coast. Much of his right wing was blown off and he ejected for the second time, having already been shot down on August 8. Despite his seat firing through the closed canopy, he survived his escape from the blazing F-105D (62-4306) and was picked up by a US Navy helicopter.

In the same flight, squadronmate 1Lt Karl Richter was assigned flak suppression with CBU-24s, and he went for a radar-controlled 85mm site. As he re-joined the flight, he saw the two MiG-17s pursuing Capt Malone and climbed to attack them. They spotted the maneuvering Richter and made a series of hard turns in order to face him head-on. When Richter broke away to re-engage, the MiGs headed back to Kep.

Le Quang Trung (left) and Ngo Duc Mai (right) scrambled from Noi Bai on August 17, 1966 and engaged F-105s. Trung subsequently claimed to have shot down 354th TFS/355th TFW *Wild Weasel* F-105F 63-8308 flown by Majs Joseph Brand and Donald Singer, although the USAF stated the jet was lost to AAA. Mai was later killed on June 3, 1967 when he was shot down by F-105D pilot Capt Larry D. Wiggins. (István Toperczer)

Brief encounters with MiG-17s also occurred during strikes on September 15 and 16. On the 15th the MiGs departed after seeing the F-105s jettison their bombs, and later during the same mission an attempt by the lead Thunderchief pilot to trap three MiGs between F-105 flights and attack them failed due to blocked radio contact. The F-4C MiGCAP flight – one of the first to fly with the F-105s rather than setting up MiG-blocking orbits near their bases – could not assist as it was low on fuel. From mid-1967, F-4C flights were often inserted between the F-105 flights, with an extra one at the rear to catch MiGs diving towards the back of the formation.

MiG-17 pilots were ordered to avoid engaging F-105 flights on September 16 after they had forced them to jettison their ordnance or, in the case of another flight bombing the Dap Cau Bridge, when the Thunderchiefs entered the field-of-fire of an 85mm AAA battery. However, one section led by Ho Van Quy went after the six F-105s targeting the bridge, while a second section, with ace Nguyen Van Bay in the lead, chased the eight Phantom II bomber/MiGCAP aircraft until Bay had shot down 555th TFS/8th TFW F-4C 63-7643.

The following day PLAAF MiGs almost accounted for the F-105D of Capt Mike Lanning when he inadvertently strayed across the border into Chinese airspace following the loss of his flight leader, Capt Darel Leetun (in 469th TFS F-105D 62-4280), to AAA. J-6s made two firing passes at him, prompting Lanning to use the familiar escape tactic of a low-level exit in afterburner.

Maj William Robinson and Capt Peter Tsouprake became involved in another scrap with MiGs on September 20 when their *Iron Hand* flight was attacked but no hits were scored by either side, due in part to an inoperative gunsight in one F-105 and incorrect armament switch selection in Robinson's cockpit.

Iron Hand aircraft were the focus of a much more decisive battle on September 21 when the Dap Cau Bridge was attacked again, this time by 48 F-105s from both Thai bases. The first large-scale aerial engagement of the war commenced with MiG-21 interceptions by the *Wild Weasel* flight, which had to rid itself of its Shrikes in order to attack a MiG-21 that was tailing two other F-105s. A potential MiG kill was once again frustrated by a jammed gun mechanism, and fuel shortages stopped two other F-105s from downing another MiG-21 that they had maneuvered into a trap.

ENGAGING THE ENEMY

Soon after *Rolling Thunder* attacks began the VPAF realised that it could predict the enemy's approach routes, timing and tactics. Defensive fighter orbits could therefore be established at low altitude near the target area to ambush the incoming F-105s and F-4s. Initially though, there was no previous experience to draw upon concerning the MiG-17's likely performance in fights with the far more modern US aircraft. Pilots were therefore trained to make fast, stabbing interceptions under precise GCI management and told to avoid air-to-air combat in which their few aircraft could soon be wasted.

If they were able to move in at gun range behind an F-105, pilots could use the considerable firepower of their single 37mm and twin 23mm cannon, aimed with the ASP-4NM gunsight and SRD-1 gun-ranging radar. In high-speed, low-level flight, vibration made use of the gunsight difficult, and poor harmonization often caused the cannon rounds to scatter. The big 37mm shells were very visible in flight, giving American pilots a better chance of avoiding them.

The MiG-17 pilots – four aviators divided into two elements – involved in this action successfully made no fewer than eight of the F-105 flights (a total of 32 aircraft) jettison their ordnance. 433rd TFS/8th TFW F-4C 63-7642 was hit by several shells from Vo Van Man's pursuing MiG-17, which was in turn targeted by Takhli flight leader Lt Col Robert Wayne. He closed in behind the MiG and fired two long bursts without a correct gunsight setting, witnessing the "sparkle" of hits on its right wing. Man dived into the undercast and escaped while the F-4 crew (Capt R. G. Kellems and 1Lt J. W. Thomas) headed out to sea and ejected after an engine exploded.

However, two MiG-17s were to fall that day, both to Thunderchief pilots, while Capt Glen Ammon of the 357th TFS was killed when his F-105D (62-4371) was shot down by 85mm AAA. One MiG, flown by Do Huy Hoang, had attacked a diving F-4C, which escaped. Hoang and his wingman then diverted their attention to the *Weasels*. As they followed two F-105s, they kept a weather-eye out for the smoke trails of the remaining two flight members, but saw nothing untoward.

1Lt Karl Richter, one of three F-105D pilots in "Ford" *Wild Weasel* flight flying jets armed with LAU-3/A rocket pods, and his wingman Capt Ralph Beardsley saw two MiGs attempting to close in behind their F-105F leader. Richter and Beardsley had followed the lead element, but at lower altitude and out of "sight" of North Vietnamese GCI radar. They duly accelerated in behind Hoang's MiG and Richter fired from 2,000ft – Beardsley expended 150 rounds at the second MiG-17 but without achieving any hits. Richter (in "Ford 3" F-105D 59-1766) closed in again and fired the rest of his ammunition, sawing off a section of the MiG's right wing. The wounded Hoang ejected seconds later and his MiG-17 exploded when it hit the ground, Richter, at just 23 years old, had become the youngest USAF MiG killer.

"Vegas" flight of 333rd TFS F-105Ds arrived shortly thereafter, and flight leader Maj John Brown went after a MiG-17 ahead of them, while retaining his ordnance. He damaged it with gunfire before his weapon jammed, closing to within 50ft but being unable to follow up his initial attack. The MiG pilot then made the mistake of following Brown as he broke off his pursuit and dove away, giving his wingman 1Lt Fred Wilson (in "Vegas 2," serial unknown) a chance to shoot large chunks out of the MiG, flown by Vo Van Man, which was seen to crash moments later. VPAF records claim that the aircraft was only damaged, however.

A jammed gun probably prevented a third MiG loss when the other two "Vegas" pilots pursued a camouflaged MiG-17 that had only 135 rounds fired at it before the M61A1 failed, enabling the VPAF fighter to dive to very low altitude and escape to Kep. Several more MiG-17s were seen when the next F-105s – a flak suppression flight – approached Dap Cau Bridge, although they stayed clear in order to allow a pair of MiG-21s to engage the Thunderchiefs in a steep climb. Shots were exchanged, but a

1Lt Karl W. Richter (right) of the 421st TFS/388th TFW and 1Lt Fred A. Wilson of the 333rd TFS/355th TFW both destroyed MiG-17s on September 21, 1966. These kills occurred within 35 miles of Hanoi, where pilots were particularly restricted by the Pentagon's frequently changing RoE that specified where, when and how MiGs could be attacked. Pilots were tested on the RoE weekly, and had to score 100 percent. During a typical 2.5-hours mission a MiG engagement might occupy only a couple of minutes. (USAF)

good firing opportunity was missed once again when the No. 4 aircraft (flown by 1Lt Roger Hegstrom) had to break away after firing only 125 rounds, scoring two hits on the MiG-21.

The VPAF briefly paused interceptions following the losses on September 21, with the next engagement not occurring until early October when an F-105 flight passed near the hornets' nest of Noi Bai and was attacked head-on by four MiG-17s and pursued by two others. The Thunderchief pilots used their afterburners to escape, as did the last flight in the strike force when it was intercepted twice by MiG-17s. The flak suppression flight had a closer encounter with MiG-21s, the "No. 2" F-105 pilot driving a "Fishbed" off his leader's tail. He was denied a likely kill by an M61 jam and a failed gun camera, which provided no evidence of the hits that he claimed on the MiG.

Increased use of QRC-160 jamming pods by F-105 flights from November 1966 reduced losses to SAMs, but it also required the fighters to maintain a tight "pod" formation to enable the QRC-160s to provide ECM cover for the whole flight. This restricted their freedom to maneuver, allowing only shallow turns at 15–20 degrees bank angle. Pod formation policies varied between Korat and Takhli, with the 355th TFW favoring looser formation than the 388th TFW. The lack of sufficient pods to equip F-4Cs at the time also had consequences in that Phantom II escorts could not follow F-105 strike flights into the "SAM belt" around Hanoi, leaving the strike flights more exposed to SA-2s and MiGs. This became particularly apparent in early December when MiG interceptions of F-105s increased markedly.

Conversely, these attacks gave F-105 pilots a greater chance of claiming an aerial victory. For example, on December 2 during a major attack on Phuc Yen AB's POL storage facility by the 388th TFW, a MiG-21 pilot's "Atolls" failed to guide, missing an F-105 and placing the overshooting communist fighter within range of the Thunderchief's cannon. With a "Fishbed" a mere 200ft from him, the USAF pilot was, however, foiled by the complex armament switchology – his only form of response was a simulated ramming attack. By then, the No. 4 F-105 pilot in the flight had moved into a perfect AIM-9 launching position. The only problem was that his jet was not carrying Sidewinders that day.

Minutes later, MiG-17s attacked the remaining F-105 flights, forcing them to jettison their 3,000lbs of bombs and defend themselves. Some damage was caused to one MiG, although the defenders soon returned to their bases, satisfied that they had caused wasted missions for the majority of the strike flights who had dumped their bombloads early.

POL strikes near Noi Bai on December 4 stirred up the most aggressive MiG opposition to date. During the 355th TFW's bomb run Capt Gerald Hawkins saw 16 MiG-17s approaching from his starboard side. Having expended his ordnance on target, he then headed off in search of a VPAF fighter – "I was definitely going to have a MiG. I just flat out wanted to mix it up with a MiG." He closed on a MiG-17 but his gunsight would not sustain a radar lock, and he soon found himself pursued by a flight of enemy aircraft. Hawkins made a head-on attack on another MiG and observed some hits and debris, although he soon had to break off and escape at Mach 1.15 when two MiG-17PFs began to fire at him from behind.

His other "Detroit" flight members departed separately, with Capt Ron Scott ("Detroit 2") outrunning another "MiG" that actually turned out to be fellow

"Detroit" pilot Maj Ken Bell! Ten MiGs challenged the fourth Takhli flight and two pilots fired at them, while others entered a tail-chase fight in which both sides fired guns and "Atolls" at single aircraft ahead of them without hits.

Korat aircraft were jumped by two flights of MiG-17s as they completed their bombing runs. Tran Huyen's flight went after F-105s that had targeted the Noi Bai fuel depot and fired at them as they attacked it, but the 388th TFW pilots escaped unscathed. Huyen saw more F-105s near Noi Bai and closed in on the fourth flight member, firing three bursts and claiming damage to the Thunderchief. The other MiG pilots, Truong Van Cung, Ngo Duc Mai and Hoang Van Ky, followed an F-105 flight and fired beyond effective range, although Ky claimed hits on the right wing of one aircraft.

The third MiG-17 flight, including Le Quang Trung, Le Xuan Di, Nguyen Xuan Dung and Luu Duc Sy, headed for the Doung Bridge area, where they encountered four F-105Ds that were part of a force of 40 Thunderchiefs bombing the Yen Vien railway marshaling yard – recently released as a permissible target and subjected to 96 750lb bombs from Korat aircraft alone.

The first wave had aborted due to weather problems, but "Elgin" flight had been spotted by Trung's flight, which had been waiting at low altitude. They attacked the F-105s, despite heavy AAA fire. As "Elgin 1" and "Elgin 2" (Capts Ray Bryant and McMahon) accelerated away at 600 knots, with the MiG-17s in pursuit, Capt Clint Murphy ("Elgin 3") selected "missiles" to release an AIM-9B as he maneuvered into a firing position behind the chasing MiGs. Moments later he saw that Bryant's F-105D had been hit by a 37mm shell, so he abandoned his prey, engaged afterburner and blasted past the MiGs to cover his leader.

Bryant's wingman, Maj Roy Dickey (in "Elgin 4" F-105D 62-4278), had just fired 20mm rounds into a warehouse as he completed his bombing run when he spotted Sy's MiG-17 on Murphy's tail. Both pilots were comparatively inexperienced in *Rolling Thunder* combat, but Dickey, with his gunsight still set to the 122-mil bombing mode, guessed at a lead angle and fired 670 rounds at Sy's MiG as it entered

MiG-17 pilots of the 923rd FR run to their camouflaged fighters at Kep in June 1967. In the background, a natural metal MiG-15UTI awaits its next training sortie. (István Toperczer)

a 3g turn, "stirring" his rudder to disperse the shells. Around 35 of them hit the MiG, starting a fire at the wing root that soon enveloped the rear fuselage. Dickey closed to within 700ft as the MiG spun into the ground with Sy still aboard.

Dickey then had to evade bullets from Dung's MiG, and he jettisoned all his remaining ordnance and tanks (possibly hitting the pursuing MiG) before egressing at 50ft and 600mph to re-join "Elgin" flight. VPAF pilots claimed two F-105s that day (both denied by the USAF), but the loss of Sy was acknowledged and the F-105's credibility as an air-to-air fighter was underlined once again.

The VPAF appeared in strength on December 8, directing eight MiG-21s at two Thunderchief flights led by Col "Jack" Broughton in another Noi Bai area POL mission. Heavy overcast contributed to a lack of hits by the MiGs' "Atolls," but they persisted in harassing the USAF formation until it jettisoned its ordnance and Lt Col Don Asire, 354th TFS commander, was almost certainly killed by a MiG (both MiG-17s and MiG-21s were active in the area) at low-level in F-105D 59-1725.

Another mixed force of 15 MiG-17s and MiG-21s intercepted a strike on December 13, but kept its distance from the F-105s, one of which (61-0187 of the 421st TFS) was then shot down by an SA-2 with the loss of Capt Sam Waters. The following day, the 357th TFS's Capt R. B. "Spade" Cooley became the first US pilot to be shot down by an "Atoll" when Dong Van De dived his MiG-21PF at a formation of 40 F-105s and the engine in Cooley's 60-0502 was blown up by the missile.

The massed MiG approach was used again on December 19 when 18 VPAF fighters forced three out of five strike flights to drop their ordnance early. On that occasion F-105 pilots identified lone MiG pilots, thought to be Soviet or North Korean advisors, who seemed to be passing instructions to the other MiG flights.

IRON ON IRON

The Thai Nguyen iron and steel production complex was one of North Vietnam's few major industrial targets, employing 10,000 people and occupying two square miles of terrain, but it was not approved as a target until March 10, 1967. Two days of F-105 attacks caused some damage, and the air action on March 10 resulted in awards and multiple aerial victories for aircrew from the 354th TFS.

Three MiG-17s in a "stacked" formation, in which the rear aircraft (often the flight leader) could direct the other two pilots and pick off any US fighter whose pilot had been distracted by the first two MiGs. An alternative formation of four aircraft would include a pair at around 6,000ft, following at a distance of 1.5 miles in a loose echelon to the leading pair at around 2,000ft. As with the stacked formation, the rear aircraft were often presented with the best opportunities when it came to engaging US aircraft that had become separated from their formations.

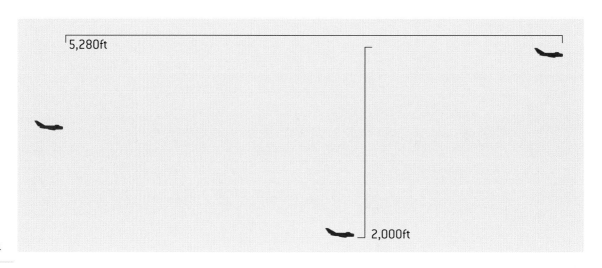

5,280ft

2,000ft

The action opened with a rear attack by MiG-21s, with other VPAF jets threatening 354th TFS mission commander Lt Col Philip Gast's "Kangaroo" flight near the target. "Kangaroo 3," Capt Max Brestel (in F-105D 62-4284), then joined Gast in the pursuit of four MiG-17s one mile ahead, with four others close behind them. Both pilots attempted to set up AIM-9s or adjust gunsights without sufficient time, resulting in Brestel simply pointing his F-105D "in the general direction of the MiG." Gast opened fire, observing sparkles on a MiG's wing as the pilots entered an intense dogfight punctuated by a SAM and AAA.

Maj Leo K. Thorsness and Capt Harold E. Johnson pose for a USAF photographer. Their one-aircraft, Medal of Honor war against ten MiGs in an attempt to rescue Majs Madison and Sterling on April 19, 1967 developed into one of the biggest aerial battles of the conflict for F-105 pilots, and resulted in four aerial victories for the 355th TFW. In Maj Thorsness' opinion, "The F-105 was a very fast airplane that could not turn." Australian slouch hats were *de rigeur* for F-105 crews, being used to mark off missions flown (applied to the hats in red ink for Route Pack 6) and record progress towards the "magic 100th" combat mission. (USAF)

Brestel fired at a MiG threatening Lt Col Gast and saw "hits in the wing, fuselage and canopy and fire in the left wing root" just before it crashed. Closing on a second MiG, Brestel observed "more hits and pieces flying off the aircraft. It appeared to be in a violent pitch-up and out of control." He was awarded confirmed victories for both MiGs, thereby becoming the first USAF double MiG killer of the war. However, the VPAF admitted only one loss, Kim Quang Wook, a "Doan Z" pilot.

On the same day the 354th TFS F-105F crew of Capt Merlyn Dethlefsen and his Electronic Warfare Officer (EWO) Capt Mike Gilroy, with wingman Maj Ken Bell, completed an *Iron Hand* mission in which they destroyed two SAM sites in several hair-raising attacks and beat off repeated pursuits by MiG-21s by flying into heavy flak and haze. Dethlefsen, who had lost his flight lead (Maj David Everson and Capt Jose Luna, in F-105F 63-8335) to 85mm AAA on their first pass, was later awarded the Congressional Medal of Honor for his bravery during the mission, with Gilroy receiving an Air Force Cross.

The next MiG to fall to an F-105 (59-1772 to be precise, which would be used by Maj Henry Higgins to down a second MiG-17 on April 28, 1967) was claimed by the highest-ranking Thunderchief pilot to achieve an aerial victory in Vietnam. On March 26, 355th TFW CO Col Robert Scott (who had claimed two victories flying P-61 Black Widows in World War II and completed 117 missions in the Korean War in the F-86) discovered several MiG-17s in the circuit at Hoa Lac airfield while on a bombing mission to a nearby target. If these jets had been on the ground, the Rules of Engagement (RoE) then in place would have prevented Scott from attacking them. However, they were very much airborne, allowing the veteran pilot to turn inside a circling, silver MiG and hit it in the left wing with multiple cannon rounds. "The last time I saw the MiG it was extremely low and rolling nose-down," Scott later recalled. Vu Huy did not eject.

April 19, in a month when attacks on MiG airfields were finally permitted in *Rolling Thunder 55*, was another exceptional day for F-105 crews. During an attack on the Xuan Mai training center for communist infiltrators by Takhli aircraft, two SA-2 sites were destroyed by 357th TFS "Kingfish" flight F-105Fs, led by Maj Leo Thorsness and his EWO Capt Harold Johnson (in 63-8301). When "Kingfish 2" (63-8341) was shot down by Nguyen Ba Dich in a MiG-17, Thorsness set up a RESCAP for its crew, Majs Thomas Madison and Thomas Sterling.

Ten MiG-17s were seen during the subsequent encounter, four of them firing S-5 unguided rockets. F-105D "Kingfish 4" sustained engine damage, but not before its (unidentified) pilot had managed to hit a MiG. He was then rescued by Capts Jerry Hoblit and Tom Wilson in "Kingfish 3," although several MiGs pursued their F-105F as it left at low altitude with no functioning afterburner. Nevertheless, they later turned back to assist with the RESCAP.

When Thorsness saw a MiG-17 heading for the parachutes of "Kingfish 2's" crew as they descended, he decided that the VPAF pilot was likely to fire at them and dived at it, expending 300 rounds as he closed on the fighter. As he got to within 100ft of his opponent he noticed "several rips in its battered left wing," and moments later Thorsness saw it "impact the ground in what appeared to be a rice field."

"Kingfish 3," meanwhile, was kept away by numerous MiG-17s and "Kingfish 4" left, its engine down on power and the pilot running low on fuel. This left Thorsness and Johnson to await the rescue force alone. After a brief exit to refuel, they returned to find a "wagon wheel" (Lufbery circle) of five MiG-17s over the area where the crew of "Kingfish 2" had landed in their parachutes. Thorsness fired his final burst of ammunition at one of them, causing extensive damage but only a "probable" kill as his gun camera was now out of film. The MiGs then intercepted the two A-1E "Sandy" RESCAP cover aircraft as they arrived on the scene and Nguyen Van Tho shot down the lead Skyraider, flown by Maj John Hamilton. Thorsness made numerous dummy passes at the MiGs to deter them until it became clear that the rescue effort had been abandoned. Both Madison and Sterling were quickly captured.

Thorsness received a Medal of Honor and Johnson an Air Force Cross following their efforts on April 19, although they had not been informed of this fact by the time they were themselves shot down and captured 11 days later.

As the strike on Xuan Mai continued, with the attacking aircraft encountering 11 MiG-17s in total, Maj Jack Hunt (in 58-1168) leading the 354th TFS's "Nitro" flight saw four enemy fighters in front of him. He quickly fired an AIM-9B at one of them, only to see the MiG pilot out-turn it. Moments later "Nitro 3," Maj Fred Tolman (in 62-4384), scared another fighter off Hunt's tail, but then had to out-run it himself when the MiG-17 pilot turned

354th TFS/355th pilot Maj Jack W. Hunt, known for his dry sense of humor, gives the photographer a thumb's up from the cockpit of his aircraft (58-1168 *Betty's Boy*) at the end of his 100th mission. Note the modest kill marking beneath the windscreen, Hunt having claimed his MiG-17 in this jet on April 19, 1967. (USAF)

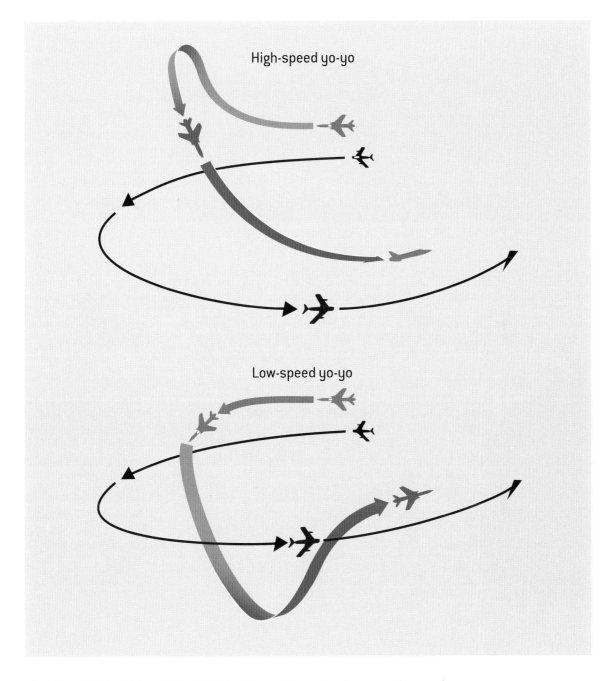

High-speed yo-yo

Low-speed yo-yo

nimbly in behind him. "Nitro" flight then reformed and returned to seek more MiGs.

Hunt followed a camouflaged example and fired 200 rounds at it, while Tolman chased another MiG-17 that was attempting to engage Hunt. It eventually flew head-on at Tolman instead, and he fired 300 rounds at the jet and observed numerous hits. When he turned to pursue it, Tolman saw white smoke and debris streaming from the aircraft. Chasing another MiG-17 instead, Tolman had just set up a textbook AIM-9 shot at his opponent against a clear blue sky when the VPAF

The high-speed yo-yo and low-speed yo-yo were aerial combat tactics used by both F-105 and F-4 pilots to compensate for the MiG-17's tighter turning circle.

pilot received a verbal warning from his wingman and turned sharply away from the Sidewinder.

Switching to his gun, Tolman claimed some damage before firing his other AIM-9 at a third MiG in a steep, climbing turn that pushed both him and his F-105D to their physical limits. Despite his exertions, and the expenditure of most of his ammunition and both of his Sidewinders, Tolman could only claim one MiG-17 destroyed. Maj Hunt was also credited with a kill after he reported seeing hits all over a MiG-17 that he dived on in his third fight of the day. Post-mission, he recalled that he had his gunsight "pipper" set "just forward and a little high on his canopy."

As Tolman and Hunt left the area, yet another F-105 flight (call sign "Panda") headed for the Xuan Mai target. Flight lead Capt Gene Eskew (in 62-4364) saw three MiG-17s in hot pursuit of the departing "Nitro" aircraft. "Panda" flight immediately cleaned off their tanks, unwittingly disqualifying themselves from subsequently providing primary RESCAP cover for "Kingfish 2," and chased the MiGs. The latter, alerted to the F-105s' presence by GCI, turned sharply. Eskew and his wingman, Capt Paul Seymour, damaged two of them, but a third MiG reversed behind the F-105s and got within gun range, forcing them to use the well-tried "afterburner escape" tactic.

They were then allowed to refuel and, as the only available aircraft, return to the "Kingfish" RESCAP effort, driving into the MiGs' attack on the two "Sandy" A-1Es at supersonic speed. A frantic line-astern chase ensued, during which the F-105D pilots severely tested their aircrafts' maneuverability limits. This in turn allowed "Sandy 2" (Capt Henry Cochran) to escape the concerted attacks by four MiG-17s.

When Eskew saw one of the MiGs break away, he followed it, firing an AIM-9B that passed within five feet of the MiG – a perfect position for detonation of the proximity fuse – without exploding. Eskew then returned to the fight in time to see "Panda 3" (Capt Howard Bodenhammer) hitting a MiG repeatedly, before he too assumed a firing position behind another VPAF fighter that was threatening "Panda 4." Eskew saw "50 to 75 hits on the upper fuselage directly behind the canopy" before pulling back hard on the stick to clear the MiG, which disintegrated in a fireball as he passed a few feet above it.

The fight continued, with both sides trading bullets and missiles in violent scissors and high-speed yo-yo maneuvers until severe fuel shortage forced Eskew to call his flight together and find a tanker. On returning to base it was found that all "Panda" gun cameras had malfunctioned, denying them two more almost certain MiG kills that could have raised the day's total to six during what had been a classic World War II-style dogfight. When Korat F-105s arrived shortly thereafter to finish off the target, no MiGs challenged them.

BASE BOMBING

The initial airfield attacks on April 24 by eight 333rd TFS F-105s reportedly destroyed 14 MiG-17s at Hoa Lac and led to strikes being mounted against all MiG-capable bases apart from Hanoi airport (Gia Lam). Many pilots wondered why it had taken so long to use this method of reducing the MiG threat, and the VPAF responded by dispersing its aircraft into camouflaged off-field shelters and caves, or flying them to China if raids were expected.

May 1967 brought six more MiG kills for F-105 pilots out of 26 credited to USAF fighters that month. Attacks on MiG bases and a policy of increasing MiGCAP flights kept VPAF fighters away and reduced bomb-jettisoning incidents, although the savage attrition by AAA and SAMs continued. Indeed, three F-105s were lost within ten minutes on May 5 during attacks on the Yen Vien marshaling yard and Ha Dong army barracks near Hanoi.

Exactly one week later, Capt Jacques Suzanne of the 333rd TFS was leading "Crossbow" flight (in F-105D 61-0159) on a flak suppression mission for a 355th TFW strike on a storage depot at Nguyen Khe when MiG-17s attempted to intervene. The ensuing action was summarized in Suzanne's victory claim statement. "My flight was trailing 'Warhawk' flight at a range of three miles, ingressing to the target. Ten miles from

the target, a flight of four MiG-17 aircraft initiated an attack on 'Warhawk.' I turned into the MiGs and tracked two MiGs that broke off to the right. I closed to 4,000ft and fired one burst of about 200 rounds. The MiGs reversed to the left, allowing me to fire another burst down to minimum range. The damaged MiG passed under my left wing trailing white smoke. The MiG crash was witnessed by 'Crossbow 01,' who saw a bright flash on the ground at the point of impact."

On May 13 no fewer than seven MiG-17s were credited to USAF fighters, five of them falling to F-105 pilots and, for the first time, two to AIM-9Bs fired from Thunderchiefs. All the MiG pilots were probably members of "Doan Z." Maj "Mo" Seaver's 90-second lethal attack (in 44th TFS/388th TFW F-105D 60-0497) on a camouflaged MiG-17 – the first VPAF jet he had ever seen – was made with a wrongly-adjusted gunsight and no time to select "missiles."

"Chevrolet" flight leader Lt Col Philip Gast (in 354th TFS/355th TFW F-105D 60-0501), faced with a head-on attack by three MiG-17s, fired his solitary AIM-9B at extreme range to distract them. He and Capt Charlie Couch (in unknown F-105D "Chevrolet 3") then resorted to guns, firing until the two flights crossed 300ft apart. Pilots in the following F-105 flight saw two MiGs going down and a pilot ejecting. Both "Chevrolet" pilots were awarded kills, and two more went to 333rd TFS/355th TFW "Random" flight pilots Majs Robert Rilling (in F-105D 60-0522) and Carl Osborne (in F-105D 62-4262). They had met two defensive "wagon wheels" of MiG-17s as they egressed, and both pilots set up Sidewinder launches. Rilling

One of the more graphic surviving gun-camera "stills" from the Vietnam War, this photograph shows a drop tank exploding under the wing of Phan Tan Duan's MiG-17 after it was hit by 20mm cannon rounds fired by Maj Ralph Kuster, who narrowly avoided colliding with the VPAF jet as it turned into a fireball and crashed on June 3, 1967. (USAF)

followed the lead MiG and his missile blew away much of its tail. As the fighter crashed, Osborne fired his AIM-9B from 4,000ft in a 1g turn and another MiG-17 began to trail smoke and descend until its tail fell off.

The MiG-17s encountered by the 388th TFW's "Hambone" flight on June 3 also used a "wagon wheel" at an altitude of just 500ft to try and trap F-105s into a formation in which they could be attacked by tighter-turning MiGs. 469th TFS pilot Capt Larry Wiggins (in F-105D 61-0069 "Hambone 3") tried to break into the circle, covered by Maj Ralph Kuster (in F-105D 60-0424 "Hambone 2") of the 13th TFS, but he overshot at 600 knots partly because his bulky centerline tank was still in place.

The MiGs re-arranged themselves in a V-formation at 200ft and Wiggins fired an AIM-9B without allowing it time to detect a heat source and emit its "growl" tone just as a MiG pilot lit his afterburner. Ngo Duc Mai, who had at least two victories to his name, saw the missile and turned, but it exploded close to his rear fuel tank, generating white vapor clouds. Wiggins followed up with 376 rounds from his 20mm cannon and the MiG exploded and crashed.

Kuster, meanwhile, had pursued Phan Tan Duan's flight-leading MiG-17 in 6g turns with an inoperative air-to-air radar mode. Duan reversed direction several times but Kuster managed to stay with him, rocking his control column in the turns to place the gunsight pipper ahead of the MiG and releasing a stream of 20mm shells at a range of just 200ft. He hit the MiG's drop tank, which exploded, strewing molten aluminum over Kuster's windscreen and streaming flames into his engine intake as the VPAF fighter rolled inverted only 25ft above the F-105 and crashed seconds later.

The MiG force had suffered heavy losses in the first half of 1967, costing it some of its most experienced pilots. Gen William Momyer, Commander, Seventh Air Force,

Capt Larry Wiggins re-enacts his June 3, 1967 MiG-17 kill with both gun and AIM-9B as "Hambone 03." Three MiG-17s were shot down that day, including one by Maj Ralph Kuster (left). Among the VPAF casualties was North Korean "Doan Z" pilot Kim The Dun. (USAF)

Two claims for Thunderchief kills were made on December 19, 1967 by Vu The Xuan (in the cockpit of MiG-17 "Red 2077" in "snake"-green camouflage) and Nguyen Phi Hung, but no US losses were recorded for that day. MiG-17 control inputs became difficult at high subsonic speeds at low altitudes, with very heavy stick forces required to induce maneuvering above 2g. It could, however, turn at 7g if the speed was kept within 300–350 knots. An F-105 pilot in a flak suppression flight noted that a MiG-17 he was pursuing completed a 150-degree turn before he had covered 25 degrees of his own turn! (István Toperczer)

declared somewhat optimistically in August that "We have driven the MiGs out of the sky for all practical purposes" and duly removed many of the F-4 MiGCAPs. They were sometimes replaced by AIM-9B-armed F-105 MiGCAP flights with their switchology "pre-set" for air-to-air mode.

However, MiGs reappeared in force for August 23 attacks on Yen Vien and Bac Giang, destroying two F-4Ds among seven losses suffered that day. 34th TFS/388th TFW pilot 1Lt David Waldrop claimed the only MiG kill after striking the target. Without a gunsight (in F-105D 61-0132), he went after a MiG-17 that was on the tail of another Thunderchief and fired until he "could see the pilot sitting in the cockpit. The whole right side of the fuselage and wing started lighting up." Le Van Phong soon ejected. Waldrop then targeted a second MiG, initially hitting it at a range of 2,500ft and then again after it briefly escaped into clouds. He saw it roll inverted into the ground. Although Waldrop initially received validation for his second kill, it was later dismissed.

"Doan Z" pilot Kim Hyun U was downed with 20mm rounds by 333rd TFS pilot Maj Donald Russell (in F-105D 62-4394) on October 18 after MiG-17s had claimed two more F-105s, resulting in an attack on Noi Bai that destroyed nine MiGs – all quickly replaced. The last F-105D kill went to 354th TFS pilot Capt Gene Basel (in 62-4284) on October 27. It was his first sighting of a MiG, and Basel hit it fatally with 20mm rounds as the MiG pilot concentrated on catching the F-105 flight ahead of him.

Two more MiG-17s were to fall in 1967, both to 357th TFS/355th TFW "Otter" flight F-105F crews on December 19. A large MiG-17 group intercepted their *Iron Hand* flight near Noi Bai, and one VPAF fighter was damaged by a MiGCAP Phantom II and finished off by Majs William Dalton and James Graham with the gun of their F-105F 63-8329. The second was destroyed minutes later by Capt Philip Drew and Maj William Wheeler (in 63-8317) with 756 rounds from their M61 cannon, thus providing them with the final F-105 MiG kill of the war.

F-105Fs were capable air-to-air fighters like their single-seat F-105D partners, and two were responsible for MiG kills on December 19, 1967. One of these aircraft was F-105F 63-8317, flown by Capt Philip M. Drew and Maj William H. Wheeler during their MiG-17 engagement on December 19, 1967. Nicknamed *Half Fast*, it carries an AGM-45A/B Shrike on its outer underwing pylon for its vital anti-SAM role. (USAF)

STATISTICS AND ANALYSIS

F-105s destroyed 27 MiG-17s and shared a 28th with a Phantom II, all within an 18-month period between June 29, 1966 and December 19, 1967. The grim total of their own losses in that period would be 126 Thunderchiefs in 1966 – the equivalent of seven squadrons of aircraft. In 1967 a further 113 were lost, at least 11 of them to MiGs, at a time when the VPAF fighter force was becoming an efficient, integrated organization containing many combat-hardened pilots. It had also learned to use the MiG-21 more effectively. Sixteen of the 24 USAF aircraft shot down in 1968 fell to MiG-21s.

The USAF Phantom II squadrons' total of 107.5 MiG shoot-downs was achieved over a much longer period between July 10, 1965 and January 7, 1973. However, at several points in 1966–67 the Thunderchief wings' success rate against MiG-17s exceeded that of the F-4 units, with 27.5 destroyed compared with 21 by F-4s in the same 18-month period, but F-4s also accounted for 21 MiG-21s. As the F-105 pilots' role was to concentrate on their bomb-runs and, in the words of MiG killer G. I. Basel, "we avoided enemy fighters if we could," these figures are impressive.

In many cases, though, MiG-17 GCI avoided the F-4 MiGCAPS (which many F-105 pilots felt were located too far from the strike flights) and went straight for the Thunderchiefs instead, occasionally becoming involved in fights with them when the F-105s had bombed and could go "air-to-air." The 388th TFW's Operations Instructions stated that if VPAF fighters appeared, "The escort flight of F-4s will first deploy to engage the attacking MiGs. Once the escort flight has engaged or has been separated for any reason, the strike force will assume its own escort responsibility. The strike force may move into a diamond formation, with No. 4 flight assuming escort responsibilities. This escort flight still has the primary responsibility of bombing the target, but it is authorized to jettison ordnance and then engage for the purpose of aiding the rest of the force to hit the target."

Alternatively, the F-105s maintained a "box" formation and the two rearmost flights became escorts, one for each side of the strike force. A perceived weakness in the use of F-4 MiGCAPs was the principle of keeping the four-ship flight intact so that the leader had to take all four members with him to fend off a MiG, leaving the Thunderchiefs vulnerable to others.

Successful fighter pilots Luu Huy Chao, Le Hai, Mai Duc Toai and Hoang Van Ky of the 923rd FR pose in front of MiG-17F "Red 2039." According to VPAF records, Le Hai and Mai Duc Toai each shot down an F-105 in dogfights during April 1967, although neither of their victories were corroborated by USAF loss records. Between them, this quartet claimed at least five Thunderchiefs destroyed. (István Toperczer)

After the final F-105 MiG kills of the campaign on December 19, 1967, 34 more Thunderchiefs were lost in 1968, but only three were attributed to MiGs. There were no more losses to VPAF fighters until Majs William Hansen and James Padgett of the 17th *Wild Weasel* Squadron were shot down in F-105G 62-4424 "Icebag 1" near Hanoi by Ngo Duy Thu's MiG-21 on May 11, 1972. Increased use of F-4 MiGCAPs had helped to deter MiGs from Thunderchief strike flights, and VPAF activity diminished generally from April 1968.

F-105 production had ended in January 1965, and heavy attrition (393 Thunderchiefs were lost in Southeast Asia to all causes out of a total production run of 753 F-105D/Fs) hastened the withdrawal of these models. They were replaced by F-4E Phantom IIs in the 388th TFW at Korat in late 1969, while the 355th TFW was inactivated at Takhli on October 10, 1970.

MiG tactics throughout *Rolling Thunder* prioritized the disruption of F-105 attacks by forcing American pilots to jettison their ordnance and defend themselves, thereby substantially negating the strike effort. As 1966 progressed, GCI became more adept at steering the MiG-17s into favorable firing positions on the strikers. Increasingly large MiG-17 interception groups of more than 15 aircraft were launched against several strikes in mid-December 1966, closely coordinated with SAM and AAA batteries to maximize the threat and distraction to USAF pilots. These tactics also reduced the F-105 pilots' opportunities to engage their attackers without breaking up their own formations, losing ECM pod integrity and exposing single aircraft to attack by MiG-21s from high altitude.

From May 1967 a modified approach placed one MiG-17 as "bait" while the other three flight members awaited the chance to pounce from behind. MiG controllers also had accurate intelligence on the direction and timing of the attacks, sometimes assisted by reports in the US press regarding future targets. They also knew that the US policy of re-attacking targets which had not been sufficiently damaged to the satisfaction of

Pentagon planners meant that a follow-up strike force's routes, timing and target were foregone conclusions for Hanoi.

The MiG interception of an *Iron Hand* flight before they reached their SAM-site targets on December 5, 1966 and the consequent loss of 421st TFS pilot Maj Burriss Begley occurred during a re-attack on the previous day's Yen Vien railway marshaling yard target. It continued to be targeted through to mid-December, often in conditions of poor visibility and with the loss of another F-105 from the 421st and Capt Sam Waters on December 13. Many other targets were similarly re-attacked with consequent Thunderchief losses.

Changes in MiG tactics late in 1966 took advantage of the increasing use of defensive "pod formations" by F-105 flights carrying QRC-160 jamming pods, which duly restricted their ability to maneuver. In looser "pre-pod" formations, the wingmen had been used to overcome the F-105's lack of rearward visibility by maneuvering gently to look out for MiGs behind them. VPAF GCI kept MiGs at low altitude, where they could not be seen by USAF radar surveillance aircraft, prior to vectoring them upwards through thin, masking cloud into the blind spot below and behind the strike formation. The MiGs also adopted a trail formation for these attacks so that if the lead VPAF jet was seen approaching and the F-105s turned to avoid it, two other MiGs closing with one-mile separation could pursue and attack the formation unseen.

In December 1966 the increase in the number of MiG engagements was dramatic, with 90 percent of them involving F-105 formations as *Rolling Thunder* began to move closer to Hanoi. At the same time, SAM and AAA defenses increased and became more concentrated around Hanoi and Haiphong as the attacks started to hit genuine strategic targets like the Yen Vien and Gia Lam railway marshaling yards close to central Hanoi. VPAF GCI limited their charges' exposure to US fighters by launching larger numbers of MiGs, as they did on December 13, 1966, and then telling them to break away if the F-105s or F-4s started to follow them. Aggressive interceptions at that point were made mainly by MiG-21s diving from well above the strike formation at supersonic speed and launching "Atolls," before accelerating away. By mid-1967 F-4 MiGCAPs had become increasingly effective, destroying six out of 14 MiG-17s and MiG-21s during one May 20 F-105 strike.

F-105D 61-0198 of the 357th TFS/355th TFW is about to resume "pod formation" after refueling in December 1966. The four-aircraft formation was flown to maximize the effect of QRC-160-1 ECM pods, single examples of which can be seen on the outer underwing pylons of both jets. This aircraft was lost during a flak suppression mission on May 5, 1967 and its pilot, 1Lt James Shively, was captured. (USAF)

By January 1967 Thunderchief pilots and WSOs were facing the most intense, multi-layered air defenses ever employed in aerial warfare. Despite this, the USAF had flown 44,500 attack sorties over North Vietnam in the previous year, delivering more than 70,100 tons of ordnance at the cost of 217 aircraft, including 126 F-105s. Combined with the realization that *Rolling Thunder* had not diminished the North's activities in South Vietnam (in fact the number of Viet Cong and North Vietnamese troops in the South had increased from 40,000 to 128,000), the credibility of the whole campaign was questioned. However, the government exposed its courageous aircrew to increasingly hostile conditions for two more years without significantly relaxing the restrictive RoE that put them at unnecessarily great risk and prevented them from deploying their capability effectively. The refusal to allow attacks on MiG airfields (partly because of resident Soviet, Chinese or North Korean personnel) was a prime example.

President Johnson's policy of frequent bombing pauses in the vain hope of negotiated settlements allowed the North to repair their military facilities, move their supplies southwards and reinforce their defenses so that pilots frequently had to return to familiar targets that they had previously devastated, to be greeted by even more fierce opposition. By November 1968, 28 percent of all F-105 pilots had been lost since 1965, and in mid-1967 the chances of successfully completing 100 missions had fallen to 50 percent. In one three-month period that year the 357th TFS lost 17 pilots.

When commanders were allowed to use their ingenuity rather than following Washington's unvarying tactics, Hanoi's defenses could be outwitted. The USAF's first two MiG-17 kills in July 1965 were enabled by substituting four missile-armed F-4Cs for the last flight in an F-105 strike force – a prelude to Operation *Bolo* on January 2, 1967. MiG pilots were usually vectored onto the last F-105 flight, but on this occasion they had to face the Phantom II's AIM-9B missiles and two "Fresco-Cs" and their pilots, Pham Thanh Nha and Nguyen Cuong, were lost.

Several pilots from the 923rd FR walk out to their MiG-17Fs (in overall gray or thinly applied dark green camouflage) in front of the earth revetments at Kep in April 1967. VPAF pilots often had a national flag attached to their parachute packs which they would unfurl if they had to bail out, thereby hopefully avoiding being shot at by their fellow countrymen as they descended. Some pilots had previously died from such "friendly" fire, and many American pilots were hit by small-arms fire as they parachuted down. (István Toperczer)

When attacks on VPAF airfields – long advocated by commanders as the quickest way to remove the MiG threat – were finally sanctioned in April 1967, some ingenious practices were devised by the 354th TFS tactical consultant and weapons officer, Maj Fred Tolman, assisted by Maj Ken Bell. Known as "offensive withdrawal," it involved concerted attacks on targets of opportunity such as MiGs or AAA/SAM batteries on the exit routes from targets. Some energetic duels with MiG-17s ensued for Tolman on April 19, which should have added two more victories to the kill he had achieved earlier in the mission had his efforts not been frustrated by AIM-9B failures.

The M61A1 gun could be an extremely accurate and reliable weapon. Lt Col Arthur Dennis of the 357th TFW saw an AIM-9B with a good launch tone wander away from the pylon of his F-105D (60-0504) and disappear unguided rather than homing onto the MiG-17 he was following on April 28, 1967. He switched to "guns" and began firing at 3,000ft and 550 knots. By the time he had closed to 700ft the MiG was a ball of fire.

Lt Col Arthur Dennis was at the controls of this F-105D, 60-0504, on April 28, 1967 when he used the aircraft's cannon to claim a MiG-17 destroyed. Delivered to the 36th TFW in October 1961, it arrived at Takhli RTAFB in March 1967 following service with the 4th, 18th and 23rd TFWs. MiG killer Capt Thomas Lesan claimed another (unconfirmed) "Fresco-C" in it later in 1967. The jet was eventually nicknamed *Memphis Belle II*, as seen here, these markings being reinstated when it was placed on display within the National Museum of the USAF at Wright-Patterson AFB, Ohio, in 1990. (USAF)

When fired within its correct, limited parameters, both AIM-9B and "Atoll" (the Soviet copy) could be devastating, as Maj Thorsness and Capt Johnson found when Le Trong Huyen's missile exploded in the tailpipe of their "Carbine" F-105F (62-4447) after the VPAF pilot had climbed unseen below them while they focused on launching a Shrike. Thorsness recalled the impact as, "like we had been smacked by a giant sledgehammer," forcing the crew to eject at 690mph on their 93rd mission. 1Lt Bob Abbott in "Carbine 4" (F-105D 59-1726) was also brought down by an "Atoll" for the first of nine kills credited to VPAF ace Nguyen Van Coc.

Although the majority of F-105 engagements and all MiG kills involved MiG-17s, there were several occasions when pilots came close to adding MiG-21 "notches" to the Thunderchief's "totem pole" in return for the 14 F-105s known to have been shot down by "Fishbeds" compared with only seven officially acknowledged by the USAF as having fallen to MiG-17s. In most cases these attempts were frustrated by weapons-switching delays, gun jams or even lack of an on-board AIM-9B. There were also recurrent gunsight problems.

For example, 333rd TFS pilot Capt Tom Lesan, leading "Rattler" flight (in F-105D 60-0498) on April 30, 1967 outpaced three MiG-17s in order to reach the target before them and then re-set his gunsight for "air-to-air." He was able to set the No. 2 MiG on fire at 1,000ft with a 100-round burst, but his aim had to be estimated using his pitot boom for guidance when his gunsight "pipper" moved right off the combining glass of the sight in a 4g turn, thus indicating that he should not fire! Lesan's wingman saw the MiG-17 spin into the ground.

Many pilots replacing the veterans of World War II or the Korean War in F-105 units in the early months of the conflict drew attention to the lack of air combat maneuvering (ACM) training they had received. The McConnell AFB course provided only five ACM sorties, and some pilots entered combat with even less preparation. F-105 pilots encountering MiG-17s for the first time were invariably amazed at the jet's frustrating ability to turn rapidly enough to get on a Thunderchief's tail almost before its pilot had time to react. As Capt Gene Eskew commented after losing a perfect firing opportunity on a MiG that turned away at the crucial moment, "It was absolutely impossible for us to follow them through that turn."

MiG pilots soon learned to use "that turn" to evade the AIM-9B, with its very limited maneuverability and field of infra-red vision, as did F-105 pilots who often had to out-maneuver the "Atoll." Maj "Hank" Higgins of the 357th TFS was one of many pilots who managed to perform the complex setting-up procedure to fire an AIM-9 at a MiG they were pursuing, only to see his opponent easily evade the missile as soon as its corkscrew smoke trail became visible. Higgins (in F-105D 59-1772) resorted to his gun moments later when he destroyed another MiG-17 instead.

He and his wingman could also be grateful for the inaccuracy of the MiG-17's gun harmonization, as they had been fired at by no fewer than ten "Fresco-Cs" during the engagement but received no damage. MiG-21 pilots used guns for only one of their successes against F-105s – the loss of 44th TFS F-105D 58-1151 and its pilot, Capt Franklin Caras, on April 28, 1967. Twenty-two others fell to "Atolls," usually fired in slashing, supersonic attacks against unsuspecting F-105 targets. MiG-17 GCI excelled in adapting and developing "aerial guerrilla" tactics of that sort, VPAF controllers knowing that they were at a disadvantage in most straight engagements with American fighters. This in turn meant the MiG regiments tended to suffer significant losses when they tried to intercept USAF strike formations with large numbers of fighters. In fact, the large-scale fights in May and June 1967 were the only times that they attempted such major confrontations during *Rolling Thunder*.

F-105 pilot Ed Rasimus wrote that fellow aviator Bill Ricks kept a journal which showed that, in the six months he had been at war, Korat had lost the equivalent of a whole wing (four squadrons) of Thunderchiefs, and that of the first class of "universally assignable" pilots, 15 out of 16 had been lost. F-105 pilots shot down about 20 percent of all the 135 MiGs claimed by the USAF in Vietnam, the others being attributed mainly to F-4 crews. However, the price paid by Thunderchief units for this success was a high one both in terms of the 21 F-105s shot down by MiG-17s and MiG-21s, and the many missions during which VPAF fighters forced a large section of the strike force to waste its ordnance before reaching the target.

FURTHER READING

BOOKS

Anderton, David, *Republic F-105 Thunderchief* (Osprey Air Combat, 1983)

Barron, William, *Crew Chief, Be He Ne'er So Vile* (Amazon, 2018)

Basel, Gene I., *Pak Six* (Associated Creative Writers, 1982)

Bell, Kenneth H., *100 Missions North* (Brassey's US/Maxwell MacMillan, 1993)

Broughton, Jack, *Thud Ridge* (J. B. Lippincott Company, 1969)

Broughton, Jack, *Going Downtown* (Orion Books, 1988)

Broughton, Jack, *Rupert Red Two* (Zenith Press, 2007)

Campbell, J. and M. Hill, *Roll Call – Thud* (Schiffer Publishing, 1996)

Colvin, J., *Twice Around the World* (Leo Cooper, 1991)

Cook, Lt Col Pete, *Takhli in Color – Life on an F-105 base during the Vietnam War* (Amazon, 2015)

Davies, Peter E., *Osprey Combat Aircraft 84 – F-105 Thunderchief Units of the Vietnam War* (Osprey, 2010)

Davies, Peter E., *Osprey Duel 35 – F-105 Wild Weasel vs SA-2 "Guideline" SAM* (Osprey, 2011)

Davies, Peter E., *Osprey Combat Aircraft 107 – F-105 Thunderchief MiG Killers of the Vietnam War* (Osprey Combat Aircraft, 2014)

Davies, Steve, *Red Eagles – America's Secret MiGs* (Osprey, 2008)

Davis, Larry and David Menard, *Republic F-105 Thunderchief* (Specialty Press, 1998)

Emerson, Stephen, *Air War Over North Vietnam – Operation Rolling Thunder* (Pen & Sword, 2018)

Geer, James, *The Republic F-105 Thunderchief, Wing and Squadron Histories* (Schiffer Publishing, 2002)

Gordon, Yefim, *Mikoyan-Gurevich MiG-17* (Aerofax/Midland Publishing, 2002)

Gordon, Yefim and Keith Dexter, *Mikoyan MiG-21* (Midland Publishing, 2008)

Hallion, Richard P., *Osprey Air Campain 3 – Rolling Thunder 1965–68* (Osprey, 2018)

Hobson, Chris, *Vietnam Air Losses* (Midland Publishing, 2001)

Jenkins, Dennis R., *F-105 Thunderchief, Workhorse of the Vietnam War* (McGraw-Hill, 2000)

Kasler, Jim with P. D. Luckett and C. L. Byler, *Tempered Steel* (Potomac Books, 2005)

Lenski, Brig Gen Al, *Magic 100* (Turner Publishing, 1995)

McNamara, Robert S., *In Retrospect – The Tragedy and Lessons of the Vietnam War* (Times Books, 1995)

Momyer, Gen William W., *Airpower in Three Wars* (University Press of the Pacific, 1982)

Plunkett, W. Howard, *F-105 Thunderchief – A 29-Year Operational* History (McFarland and Co., 2011)

Plunkett, W. Howard, *Fighting Cavaliers – The F-105 History of the 421st Tactical Fighter Squadron, 1963–1967* (CreateSpace/Amazon, 2018)

Rasimus, Edward J., *When Thunder Rolled – An F-105 Pilot Over North Vietnam* (Smithsonian Books, 2003)

Rock, Col Edward T. (ed.), *First In, Last Out* (The Society of Wild Weasels/Authorhouse, 2005)

Thompson, Wayne, *To Hanoi and Back – The USAF and North Vietnam 1966–73* (University Press of the Pacific, 2000)

Toperczer, István, *Osprey Combat Aircraft 25 – MiG-17 and MiG-19 Units of the Vietnam War* (Osprey, 2001)

Toperczer, István, *MiG Aces of the Vietnam War* (Schiffer Military History, 2015)

Toperczer, István, *Silver Swallows and Blue Bandits, Air Battles Over North Vietnam* (Artipresse, 2015)

Toperczer, István, *Osprey Aircraft of the Aces 130 – MiG-17/19 Aces of the Vietnam War* (Osprey, 2016)

Thorsness, Leo, *Surviving Hell – A PoW's Journey* (Encounter Books, 2008)

Truong Nhu Tang, *A Viet Cong Memoir* (Vintage, 1986)

Van Staaveren, Jacob, *Gradual Failure – The Air War Over North Vietnam 1965–66* (Air Force History and Museum Program, 2002)

Vizcarra, Vic, *Thud Pilot* (Thud Pilot Productions, 2016)

Warner, Wayne A, *One Trip Too Many* (CreateSpace/Amazon, 2011)

Wilson, Tom, *Lucky's Bridge* (a novel based on the 355th TFW in Vietnam) (Bantam, 1993)

DOCUMENTARY SOURCES

388th TFW, F-105 Combat Tactics (USAF Historical Research Agency, Maxwell AFB, 1967)

Air War Vietnam; Plans and Operations 1961–68, J. Van Staaveren, H. Wolk and S. Slade, (USAF Historical Research Center Monographs)

Project CHECO Reports: Air-to-Air Encounters Over North Vietnam July 1, 1967–December 31, 1968 (HQ PACAF, August 30, 1969)

WSEG-116-Vol 1. *Air-to-Air Encounters in South East Asia. F-4 Events Prior to March 1, 1967*

WSEG-116-Vol 2. *Air-to-Air Encounters in South East Asia. F-105 Events Prior to March 1, 1967*

WSEG-116-Vol 3. *Air-to-Air Encounters in South East Asia. Events from March 1, 1967 to August 1, 1967 and Miscellaneous Events*

INDEX

Page numbers in **bold** refer to illustrations.

afterburning 15, 27
air intakes 11, 18
AP-63-FBX 10
automatic flight control system **39**
avionics 10, **10**, 19, 25

Bay, Nguyen Van 51, **51**, 59
Blank, Maj Kenneth T. 23, 55, 58, **58**
brakes 18
Brestel, Capt Max 65
Broughton, Col "Jack" **37**, 39, 64
Byrd, Sgt Neil **39**

camouflage **14** (15), **75**
Chao, Luu Huy 44, **47**, 58, **73**
chronology 6–8
cockpits **38**, **45**
combat 50–71
    air base bombing and attacks 68–71, 75, 76
    air combat maneuvering (ACM) 77
    Bac Giang Bridge mission, 1966 50–51
    "Black Sunday," August 7, 1966 52–53
    disruption of F-105 attacks 73–74
    engaging the enemy **60**
    escort flights 72–73
    mixed MiG encounters 53–64, **54**, **56–57** (55), **58**, **59**, **63**
    offensive withdrawal tactics 76
    pod formations 62, 74, **74**
    POL storage facilities, attacks on 51–52, **51**, 54, **56–57** (55), 63
    stacked formations **64**
    Thai Nguyen complex, attack on, March 1967 64–65
    Xuan Mai training center attack 65–68
    Yen Bai munitions complex, 1966 51
    yo-yo tactics **67**
combatants
    United States 36–42
    Vietnamese 42, 44–49
Cooley, Capt Bob "Spade" 37, 39

Denton, Murray (pilot) 36–37
design and development
    F-105 Thunderchief 9–13
    MiG-17 13–16
Diamond, 1Lt Steve **54**, **54**, **56–57** (55)

engines 10, 13, 16
    J75-P-19W 17–18
    Klimov VK-1 26, **26**
    Klimov VK-1F 26–27

F-84 9–10
    F-84 Thunderjet 9
    F-84 Thunderstreak 9
F-86 Sabre 13
F-105
    cockpit **38**
    F-105A 10
    F-105B **10**, 11
    F-105B [54-0102] **11**
    F-105B 57-5836 **4**
    F-105D 13, 17, 19, **35**, **38**, **51**, **54**
    F-105D 60-0504 *Memphis Belle II* **76**
    F-105D 61-0132 *HANOI Special* **36**

F-150D-10-RE 60-0497 **12**
F-105F 17, 52–53, **53**
F-105F 63-8317 **71**
F-105G 17
    losses 4–5, 35, 41, 46, 48, 49, 50, 52–53, 54, 58, 59, 64, 69–71, 72, 73, 74, 75, 77
    maintenance 39–40, **40**
    nicknames **29**
    performance 11, 36–37
    Thunderchief, design and development of 9–13
    Thunderchief, technical specifications 17–25
    Two-seaters 13
    withdrawal of 73
    YF-105A 11, **11**
    YF-105A, 54-0099 **6**
    YF-105B 10–11
    YRF-105B 10–11
friendly fire 48, **75**
Fuller, Capt Ben 37, 39

Gast, Lt Col Philip 65, 69
ground-controlled interception (GCI) 4–5
groundcrews 39–40, **44**

Hai, Le 44, **47**, **73**
Hanh, Tran 49, **49**
Horn, Capt Boyd Van 39
Hosmer, Bill 37
Hung, Nguyen Phi **47**, 70
Hunt, Maj Jack W. 66–67, **66**, 68

Johnson, Capt Harold E. **65**, 66, 76

Kasler, Maj James H. 39, 40, 43, **43**, 53–54
Kuster, Maj Ralph **69**, 70, **70**
Ky, Hoang Van **47**, 63, **73**

Mach 3 XF-103 10
Mai, Ngo Duc 55, **59**, 63, 70
medals and awards 39, 43, 65, 66
MiG-9 13
MiG-15 13, 15
    MiG-15UTI **16**
MiG-17 26, **32**
    cockpit **45**
    design and development 13–16
    losses 4–5, 12, 48, 52, **58**, 68, 69, **69**, 72, 75, 77
    MIG-17F "Fresco-A" "Blue 61" **7**, 26
    MIG-17F "Fresco-C" **5**, 26
    MiG-17P "Fresco-B" 16
    MiG-17PF "Fresco-D" 16, **26**
    MiG-17A **44**, **46**
    rear fuselage section **15**, 25
    Shenyang J-5 "Red 3012" **14** (15)
    technical specifications 25–28
    testing 15
    two seaters 16
MiG-21 20, 22, 29, 46, 47, 53, 54, 58, 59, 61–62, 64, 65, 72, 74, 76, 77
missions 40–41, 47–48

Nash, Capt John 5

OKB-155 design bureau 13, 15, 16
operation instructions 72–73
Operation *Rolling Thunder* 34–35, 39, 41, 42, 74, 75

P-47 Thunderbolt 9

pilots 4–5, 37, 39, 41, **47**, **48**, **63**, **73**, **75**
    training 41–42, 44, **44**, 46–47, 48, 77

Quy, Ho Van **47**, 59

radar 13, 15, 16, 27
refueling systems **11**, **18**, 19
Richter, 1Lt Karl W. 59, 61, **61**

Scott, Col Robert 65
Seaver, Maj Maurice "Mo" **12**
statistics and analysis 72–77
strategic situation 29–35
    air bases **30**, 34
    railway and bridge targets **35**
Suzanne, Capt Jacques 69

tailplane flutter 15
technical specifications
    F-105 Thunderchief 17–25
    MiG-17 25–28
Thorsness, Maj Leo **65**, 66, 76
Toai, Mai Duc **73**
Tolman, Maj Fred 55, 66–68, 76
Trung, Le Quang 55, **59**

United States Air Force units
    18th Organizational Maintenance Squadron (OMS) 40
    18th TFW 29, **29**, 31, 40
    23rd TFW **35**, 41
    36th TFS 31–32
    44th TFS **12**, 31, 32, 69, 77
    388th TFW **12**, **36**, 39, 50, 51, 52, 55, 58, 62, 63, 71, 72–73
    421st TFS 19, 41, 49, 50, 52, 58, 64, 74
    469th TFS 41, 50, 70
    562nd TFS **35**

VPAF units
    921st FR 32, **32**, 33, 47, 48, 49

water injection 17
weaponry 10
    AGM-45A/B Shrike missiles **53**
    AIM-9B Sidewinder missiles 19–22, **20**, **21**, 23, 53–54, 76, 77
    armament switches 24
    belted ammunition systems **24**
    CBU-24/B cluster bomb unit 51
    General Electric M61A1 Vulcan rotary cannon 4,13, **13**, 19, 22–23, **23**, 76
    General Electric T171 cannon **22**
    gun-ranging radar 15
    gunsight problems 76–77
    K-13 Atoll 22, 46, 53, 64, 74, 76, 77
    K-19 reflector gunsight 23
    M118 GP "bridge busters" **19**
    nuclear stores **11**, 19
    Nudel'man N-37D cannon 27–28, **27**, **28**
    Nudel'man-Rikhter NR-23 **16**, 28
    QRC-160A ECM pods **21**
    removing/replenishing ammunition **25**
Wiggins, Capt Larry 59, 70, **70**
Wilson, 1Lt Fred A. 25, 61, **61**
wings 25
    swept-wing technology 13, 15, 18